# BRIGHT NOTES

# NARCISSUS AND GOLDMUND BY HERMANN HESSE

## Intelligent Education

Nashville, Tennessee

BRIGHT NOTES: Narcissus and Goldmund
www.BrightNotes.com

No part of this publication may be used or reproduced in any manner whatsoever without written permission, except in the case of brief quotations in critical articles and reviews. For permissions, contact Influence Publishers http://www.influencepublishers.com.

ISBN: 978-1-645422-12-9 (Paperback)
ISBN: 978-1-645422-13-6 (eBook)

Published in accordance with the U.S. Copyright Office Orphan Works and Mass Digitization report of the register of copyrights, June 2015.

Originally published by Monarch Press.
E.S. Friedrichsmeyer, 1972
2020 Edition published by Influence Publishers.

Interior design by Lapiz Digital Services. Cover Design by Thinkpen Designs.

Printed in the United States of America.

Library of Congress Cataloging-in-Publication Data forthcoming.
Names: Intelligent Education
Title: BRIGHT NOTES: Narcissus and Goldmund
Subject: STU004000 STUDY AIDS / Book Notes

# CONTENTS

1) Introduction to Hermann Hesse     1

2) Introduction to Narcissus and Goldmund     18

3) Textual Analysis
   - Chapter One     28
   - Chapter Two     32
   - Chapter Three     35
   - Chapter Four     37
   - Chapter Five     42
   - Chapter Six     46
   - Chapter Seven     49
   - Chapter Eight     52
   - Chapter Nine     54
   - Chapter Ten     56
   - Chapter Eleven     59
   - Chapter Twelve     63
   - Chapter Thirteen     66
   - Chapter Fourteen     69
   - Chapter Fifteen     71
   - Chapter Sixteen     74
   - Chapter Seventeen     77
   - Chapter Eighteen     80

| | |
|---|---|
| Chapter Nineteen | 83 |
| Chapter Twenty | 85 |

4) Character Analysis — 88

5) Criticism — 100

6) Essay Questions and Answers — 107

7) Topics for Research and Criticism — 116

# HERMANN HESSE

## INTRODUCTION

### FAMILY BACKGROUND

Like many German writers, Hermann Hesse came from a family which had for many generations been associated with the Protestant clergy. The father, Johannes Hesse, was a protestant clergyman who belonged to the pietistic tradition, a liberal branch of German Protestantism which stressed a concern for the individual's relationship to God above strict formal dogma. Hermann was later to acknowledge the importance of the religious atmosphere of his childhood, as, for example, in a letter dated 1950 in which he spoke of Christianity as it was lived, rather than preached, in his home. Johannes Hesse spent the years 1869 to 1873 as a missionary in India. There he acquired an interest in Oriental philosophy and theology which he was to retain for the rest of his life. Forced to return to Europe on account of poor health, he settled in Calw, a town in Southwestern Germany, where he was active as an author of works on religious subjects. Hermann's mother, Marie, came from a similar background; she had been in India as the wife of a missionary. She was living in Calw after the death of her first husband when she met Johannes Hesse.

Hermann, the second of six children, was born in Calw on July 2nd 1877. Four years later the family moved to Basel, Switzerland, and acquired Swiss citizenship. The father continued his religious work in Basel where he became the editor of a missionary magazine. In 1886 the family returned to Calw where Hesse was to remain until leaving home to attend a boarding school in 1890. Hermann's early childhood years were for the most part pleasant and they were certainly intellectually stimulating. Literature, philosophy, and the arts were discussed and respected in his home. Guests, many of whom came from foreign lands, were often entertained there. Hermann felt an especial affinity to his mother whose loving care provided him with a feeling of security and well-being. His father, on the other hand, in spite of his tolerance in regard to many theological matters, believed in strict discipline and followed rigid theories of education which allowed no room for freedom of expression on his son's part. Many of the difficulties of these early years are reflected in Hesse's works, as, for example, in "A Child's Heart." As a boy, Hermann was not an outstanding pupil and did not enjoy school; he once remarked that he had had only one teacher whom he admired.

## SEARCH FOR A CAREER

As was common in Germany at that time, Hermann was sent to a boarding school to prepare for the difficult examination which all students had to pass in order to be admitted to advanced schools and the university. He entered the school in Goppingen in 1890 to undertake this preparation. At this school, for the only time in his life, he was an exceptionally good student. After successfully passing the examination, he followed the wishes of his father and enrolled in the famous school at Maulbronn with the intention of becoming a Protestant minister. The atmosphere of the school soon proved too oppressive and Hermann ran away. He returned, but once more was unable to adjust and soon left the school permanently. The months which followed were exceedingly traumatic for the disturbed youth. Help was sought from various persons and institutions, but Hermann's emotional problems could not be alleviated. Once he even went so far as to attempt suicide. His final exposure to formal education was at a preparatory school in Bad Cannstatt in 1893 and 1894. Hesse was not at all happy there and his experiences formed the basis for the descriptions of some of Sinclair's unhappy school experiences in *Demian*.

While doing mechanical work in a Calw clock factory in 1894 and 1895, the young Hesse decided that he wanted to become a writer. He soon found employment i a bookstore in Tubingen and began to see meaning, or at least potential meaning, in life. In 1899 he published his first books, a collection of poetry and one of short prose pieces. In that same year he moved to Basel where he continued to work in the book trade and to expand his horizons, by reading books of many different kinds, and by traveling in Switzerland and Italy. Two years later he wrote a book which attracted the attention of some important German critics and which accordingly established Hesse's reputation as an author: *The Posthumous Papers and Poems of Hermann Lauscher*.

## IMPORTANT EARLY WRITINGS

Other books followed, including, in 1904, the novel *Peter Camenzind*. This book was immediately successful and the royalties from it and from other writings gave Hesse a degree of financial independence. He was accordingly able to leave the book trade and devote himself entirely to his writing. The novel is about a poor but talented Swiss boy who grows up in harmony with nature, but decides to go out into the world where he eventually attains a measure of material success in society. He ultimately comes to realize that he has not found self-fulfillment in love, intellectual pursuits, art, music, or material goods. Following the death of his close friend Boppi, a cripple, he finally retires to lead an isolated life free of the demands of society. Already in the first of Hesse's novels we see very clearly the **theme** that will pervade all of the later ones: the difficult search on the part of an individual for identity and fulfillment.

Hesse soon became a respected member of the German literary elite and contributed stories, poems, reviews, and essays to many of the leading periodicals of that time. He also continued to write novels and the next one, *Beneath the Wheel* (1906), was to a great extent autobiographical. It relates the unsuccessful attempt of the hero, Hans Giebenrath, to cope with the stifling atmosphere of the educational system. The two sides of Hesse's own nature are shown in Hans and in Hermann Heilner, who rebelled against the system and ran away. Hans, like Hesse, experienced many disappointments and eventually found himself unable to cope with the demands of his father and of the school. In two very important respects, however, the novel does not follow Hesse's biography; Hans' mother dies when he is very young, depriving him of a source of warmth and love, and Hans himself, in a state of depression, drowns while still a young man. One of many German literary works of the early twentieth century which attacked the educational system, *Beneath the Wheel* was very popular.

Hesse's next two novels, *Gertrude* (1910) and *Rosshalde* (1914), deal with the problems of the artist. The former is one of the least autobiographical of Hesse's works. The hero, Kuhn, is a musician who enjoyed a happy childhood. He injures his leg in an accident and becomes introverted. He falls in love with Gertrude, but lacks the self-assurance to reveal his feelings to her and try to win her love. She marries another man, but the marriage is not successful and her husband commits suicide. Kuhn becomes a great composer, although he remains a lonely and unhappy person. He has limited contact with Gertrude in his later years, although she continues to be a source of inspiration for his great works of art.

## YEARS OF CRISIS

In Hesse married Maria Bernoulli, a Swiss woman nine years his elder. The couple led an isolated life in Gaienhofen. Sons were born in 1905 and 1909. Hesse was a successful and highly productive writer, but his marriage became progressively less happy. In 1911 he made a journey to the Orient in the company of the painter Hans Sturzenegger. Hesse was particularly interested in India, the country in which both of his parents had lived and which his father and grandfather had studied extensively. The trip, however, did not enable Hesse to find the peace and fulfillment which he so desperately sought. Some of his impressions are recorded in From India (1913). His personal conflicts are reflected rather directly in the novel *Rosshalde,* the story of the painter (1904) Johann Veraguth, who lives a lonely and unhappy life at his estate, *Rosshalde,* with his wife and a younger son, Pierre. An older son, Albert, is away at school and returns only during vacation periods. Life acquires meaning for Veraguth through his work as an artist and his love for Pierre. He tolerates his marriage only for the sake of Pierre. What remains of his happiness is shattered when Pierre dies of meningitis. The end of the novel remains open. Veraguth, turning his back on bourgeois society, leaves *Rosshalde* and his wife to travel. His future is uncertain.

The outbreak of World War I in 1914 marked another crisis in Hesse's complicated personal life. Although he had been living in Switzerland for many years, he was German and his reading public expected him to support the German cause. (Switzerland remained neutral during the war.) Hesse did not immediately assume an anti-German stand, but he publicly questioned the excessive patriotism in his native country which was brought out by the war and he was in turn sharply criticized from many sides in Germany. He remained in Switzerland throughout the war and was active in the effort to improve the lot of German prisoners of war and internees.

Hesse's literary productivity continued undiminished during the first years of the war and *Knulp*, one of the more popular of his earlier works, appeared in 1915. The three stories contained in the collection will be analyzed in detail in this *Monarch Note*.

The following year, 1916, was to bring severe misfortune: the death of his father, the serious illness of his son Martin, and the mental breakdown of his wife, who had to be sent to an institution. This was in fact the end of Hesse's first marriage, although he did not obtain a formal divorce until 1923. Hesse was naturally despondent and his search for psychiatric help brought him in contact with Dr. Joseph Lang, a disciple of the eminent psychologist Carl Gustav Jung. From Doctor Lang, Hesse not only received advice which helped him overcome his own personal crisis, but he also learned in detail the theories of Jung. Hesse became a devoted student of Jung and the influence of this psychologist was to become one of the most important factors in his later works.

## THE MIDDLE YEARS

*Demian* was written during a short period of time in 1917 under the immediate influence of Doctor Lang and, through him, of Jung. This new novel marks a radical break in Hesse's literary development and the author did not want his readers in any way to be reminded of his earlier works or to associate the new Hesse - the Hesse of *Demian* - with them. Accordingly he published the novel in 1919 under the pseudonym Emil Sinclair, the name of one of the main characters of the book. The novel was an immediate success. The young postwar generation felt a strong affinity to this strange, powerful work, and it was also well-received by literary critics. The Fontane Prize, a prestigious literary prize awarded for outstanding first novels, was presented to the mysterious Emil Sinclair. The prize was returned by the publisher and in 1920 Hesse revealed that he was actually the author. But he had achieved his goal. To the reading public, Hermann Hesse was now primarily known as the author of *Demian,* not of *Peter Camenzind*, *Rosshalde,* and other early works which Hesse had come to consider to be immature.

The most important **theme** of *Demian* is the necessity of first recognizing, and then integrating into one's personality, the two different aspects of life - the "light" and the "dark," the spiritual and the sensual, saintliness and sin. The setting, plot, and style of *Demian* are for the most part dissimilar from those of Hesse's previous works. It is set in Germany during the early years of the present century and describes the outer and inner development of Emil Sinclair from late childhood to maturity. Here, as in *Siddhartha, Narcissus and Goldmund*, and many of Hesse's works - although not in the stories discussed in this Monarch Note - three distinct stages of development can be seen: the early period of innocence, a middle period which is not without searching, loneliness, and even despair, and the final period in which a synthesis is effected. When Emil Sinclair is first introduced to the "dark" world, he sees no way to reconcile the warm, serene atmosphere of his home with the cold frightening world he now sees. But with the help of Max Demian he gradually becomes more and more able to see the possibility of accepting both aspects of his human nature and he eventually finds he is no longer forced to view them as polar opposites.

The year 1919 was indeed an important one. Hesse wrote several important essays during that year, including Zarathustra's Return in which his debt to Nietzsche is acknowledged, and three of his better short stories, "A Child's Heart," "Klingsor's Last Summer" and "Klein and Wagner," published together in 1920 under the title *Klingsor's Last Summer*. These three stories will be analyzed in detail in this Monarch Note. Furthermore, Hesse moved from Bern, where he had been living, to the small Swiss town of Montagnola, which was to be his home in his later years. It was also at about this time that Hesse first took up painting; he later became an accomplished painter and it was to remain his favorite hobby throughout his life. And finally, work on the next important book, Siddhartha, was begun in this year.

Siddhartha proved to be an especially difficult book to write. As Hesse remarked, the first two periods of the hero's life, those of innocence and searching, were easy for him to portray. But the final triumphant vision of the old Siddhartha was foreign to Hesse's experience and hence he had great difficulty putting it on paper. Only in 1922 was the completed novel published.

In this highly poetic book set in ancient India Hesse describes the life of Siddhartha. First the hero masters his intellect and will, and then he turns to the world of the senses. He finds neither asceticism nor hedonism totally satisfying. Late in life he finds fulfillment in a mystical vision at, and with the help of, a river, the symbol of perfection, unity, and continuity.

In 1923 Hesse became a Swiss citizen. His personal life, however, remained unsettled. He obtained a divorce from his first wife and soon thereafter (in January, 1924) he married Ruth Wenger. Five years were to lapse before the publication of his next major novel, *Steppenwolf* (1927). These years were far from totally barren. Hesse continued to publish poems, short stories, essays, and reviews in various journals and newspapers. But a feeling of alienation, which is reflected in the suffering of Harry Haller in *Steppenwolf*, continued to affect him. His second marriage, like the first, did not prove to be successful; it ended in divorce in 1927. By this time Hesse was one of the most famous writers of his generation and his first full-length biography, by Hugo Ball, appeared in conjunction with his fiftieth birthday in that same year.

*Steppenwolf,* like *Demian,* "Klein and Wagner," and "Klingsor's Last Summer," has a "realistic" setting in the twentieth century. The hero, Harry Haller, is a middle-aged man who is torn between the world of the bourgeoisie and that of the artist-intellectual. At first he believes that there are but two aspects of his personality, and that he is torn between these irreconcilable poles. He finds a mysterious "treatise" (reflecting insights of his own unconscious) which points out that his conception of a simple duality within himself was incorrect. There are not two Harry Hallers, the *Steppenwolf* and the bourgeois citizen, but many very different aspects of a complicated individual. Haller gradually comes to realize and accept this fact on a conscious level during the remainder of the novel, and the closing scene, the so-called "Magic Theater," symbolically represents the progress which he has made.

In 1930 one of Hesse's most popular novels appeared, *Narcissus and Goldmund*. Set in the Middle Ages (although not in any specific century), with a plot rich in adventure, the novel examines the duality of spirit and nature, incorporated by the two leading characters, Narcissus and Goldmund, respectively. Most of the story is devoted to Goldmund's wanderings. Originally a seminarian, he is told by his friend and teacher Narcissus that he is not destined for the priesthood. He leaves the seminary and has many adventures. He has brief, but meaningful, affairs with many women; he experiences birth and death, and is himself forced to kill another human being; and great effort he becomes a skilled sculptor and produces a few pieces of extraordinary beauty. Narcissus, on the other hand, becomes a priest and intellectual. Each respects the other, and Narcissus often helps his friend in one way or another. Although Goldmund dies a realistic and un-idealized death, his way of life, which includes both the spirit and the senses, is presented as superior to that of Narcissus, whose philosophy attempts to deny death, and who, as a result, will not be able to face death when it comes, as it inevitably must. In many respects this novel invites comparison with Knulp.

Hesse married again in 1931. His third wife, with whom he was to remain until his death some thirty years later, was Ninon Auslander Dolbin, Hesse's happiness during these years is portrayed symbolically in the highly autobiographical, but equally unrealistic, novel *Journey to the East* (1932). The hero is named "H.H.," an obvious **allusion** to Hermann Hesse, and many other references to the author's life can be detected in the book. Once again the hero goes through three stages in his development. He naively and confidently joins a secret Order or League and takes part in its "Journey to the East." He later drops out of the League and experiences intense loneliness and despair. With the help of Andreas Leo, a figure who resembles the old Siddhartha in some respects, he finally comes to understand the League, and himself, and then comes to feel a sense of harmony with the world.

For Hesse, unlike most important German-speaking writers, Hitler's rise to power in the early 1930s did not signal any radical changes. Hesse was already a Swiss citizen and although his hatred of war - and of the other things for which Nazism stood-remained undiminished, he was not and never had been a political activist. He had little faith in practical politics and hence did not join the active political opposition to the Nazis. In the early 1930s, under the dark cloud which covered Europe, Hesse began work on his last great novel, *The Glass Bead Game*, or *Magister Ludi*, as it is often called in English. According to Hesse's original plans, this work was to consist of a number of "autobiographies" which would describe successive reincarnations of a single person. Hesse's conception of the novel changed as he was writing it and the emphasis shifted to the final historical period, the world of Castalia, about the year 2400 A.D. The three autobiographies of Joseph Knecht that are appended to the novel are vestiges of the original plan, and a fourth autobiography was also written but not included in the book. As Hesse himself later stated, the writing of *The Glass Bead Game* was his own spiritual defense against the deadly political and moral climate in the world at that time.

Joseph Knecht's biographies and poems, which are appended to the narrator's dry, pedantic biography, most clearly reveal the novel's important issues and themes. Knecht comes to realize that he must seek oneness with nature, but is not able to formulate his ideas, let alone express them adequately and directly in words. He ultimately does seek that he cannot find what he is seeking in the rarified atmosphere of Castalia, and accordingly forsakes it in favor of a life in the "real" world. He dies before coming to a full conscious realization of the significance of his feelings and actions, and critics hence sometimes debate the validity of his life. But he has remained true to himself, and his life must therefore be called successful.

## OLD AGE

Hesse's reputation continued to grow after the publication of *The Glass Bead Game*. He was awarded the Nobel Prize for literature - the world's highest literary award-in 1946, and later received several other important prizes and awards in recognition of his literary work. He continued to write poetry and short prose pieces and he faithfully answered the numerous letters addressed to him by admiring readers, although he felt uncomfortable in the role of advisor and father confessor. But *The Glass Bead Game* was to be his last novel. As the years went by, he guarded his privacy more and more carefully and seldom left his secluded home at Montagnola, of which he was so fond. He died of a brain hemorrhage on August 9, 1962, a month after his eighty-fifth birthday.

## INTELLECTUAL INFLUENCES

It would be impossible even to list all of the important influences on Hesse. He was exposed to theology, philosophy, literature, and the other arts at an early age and retained his varied interests throughout his long life. Among the literary figures whom he most admired, however, two deserve particular mention: the mystical Romantic poet Novalis (pseudonym of Friedrich von Hardenberg, 1772-1801), and Johann Wolfgang von Goethe (1749-1832), about whom Hesse once said: "Among all German writers, Goethe is the one to whom I owe the most, the one to whom I am most deeply indebted, who has held my attention, enslaved and encouraged me, forced me to follow his lead or vigorously attack it." Hesse also knew many religious and philosophical writers. As was mentioned above, Christianity was quite important as a formative influence. He also studied various Eastern religions in some depth.

Two of the most important influences on Hesse's thought must be discussed here: the philosopher and poet Friedrich Nietzsche (1844-1900) and the psychologist Carl Gustav Jung (1875-1961). Before going into the extent of these influences, however, it must be emphasized that individuality remained one of Hesse's fundamental values. He read Nietzsche and Jung, as well as Goethe, Novalis, Dostoevski, Freud, and other great writers, but always with a critical eye. Although Hesse did not imitate Nietzsche, Jung, or anyone else, an understanding of certain basic concepts of Nietzsche and Jung can facilitate the approach to some of Hesse's difficult works.

Nietzsche and Jung share some important beliefs which are also to be found in the works of Hesse. Perhaps the most important of these is the insistence upon the necessity of finding one's own path toward self-realization, and of accepting the dark, so-called "sinful" side of human nature in the process. Nietzsche called for a complete revaluation of moral standards entirely eliminating the Judeo-Christian morality which he felt represented a philosophy that valued weakness and conformity rather than strength and individuality, which he preferred. Hesse, too, continually rejects weakness and conformity. The concept which Nietzsche called amor fati ("Love of fate") is likewise shared by Hesse. This concept refers to a joyful acceptance of the world as it is; it is a highly affirmative philosophy, and variations of it can be seen in Klingsor and Klein.

Jung, in more practical terms, refers to the inferior, animalistic side of our nature as the "shadow," and warns against the bad effects of simply attempting to repress it. This part of our human nature must rather be first understood, and then accepted, he maintains. Other of Jung's concepts are also useful in understanding Hesse, especially those of the "unconscious" and the "archetype." Jung believes that a large body of experiences remain in a person's unconscious (he objects to Freud's term "subconscious," which seems to him to carry derogatory implications). Each individual has elements which are part of his "personal unconscious"; that is, memories and emotions from his past which have been removed from his immediate conscious memory, but which may still exert an important and even decisive effect on his behavior unconsciously. There are also elements of the unconscious which are shared by everyone. Jung studied ancient symbols and myths, and analyzed the dreams of his contemporaries. He came to the conclusion that many symbols recur even though modern man may not have known of the ancient representations. Such symbols which have universal significance are said by Jung to be part of the "collective unconscious," and are called "archetypes."

Finally, Jung coined the term "anima" to refer to an unconscious feminine aspect within a man through which he can to some extent intuitively comprehend the nature of women. The references in *Demian* to masculine traits in a woman, or feminine traits in a man, are based on this concept, and many apparent **allusions** to homosexuality, which some critics are fond of pointing out, can likewise be explained on the basis of Jung's concept. The several aspects of personality, in Jung's formulation, must be integrated if a person, man or woman, is to attain fulfillment. They must accordingly always be considered as parts of a whole, and not as isolated components.

## HESSE'S POPULARITY

The history of Hesse's popularity in Germany and America is complex and, on the surface at least, enigmatic. He was a competent popular novelist and essayist during the first two decades of this century and enjoyed a certain following among the German reading public at that time. Upon the publication of *Demian* in 1919, he immediately became one of the heroes of one segment of the younger generation in Germany. His disillusionment with the war and his visionary, even mystical attitude toward the future contributed greatly to his popularity and to his success (although it should be noted that some Germans reproached him for his lack of patriotism during the war). His popularity in German-speaking countries remained high until the early 1930s, when Hitler assumed power in Germany. Because they were largely unpolitical, Hesse's books were not immediately burned and banned in Germany, but his work was not encouraged or even approved by the Nazi hierarchy. Many important intellectuals and writers, both German and non-German, praised Hesse highly. Among these are T.S. Elliot, Andre Gide, and Thomas Mann. After a brief period of popularity in Europe following the Second World War, Hesse's reputation began to decline, both among academicians and the younger generation of readers. At the present time, Hesse's reputation in Germany is at an all-time low. The young radicals, especially, have no use for his writings since they associate them with the Romantic past - including Nazism! - which they desire to overcome and leave behind.

Hesse has been widely translated into non-European languages, and his reception in India and Japan, especially, has been consistently favorable, and not subject to the ups and downs which mark his popularity in Germany and in America. Hesse was proud of the fact that readers in Eastern countries appreciated his works, which contain many elements of Eastern philosophy.

The history of Hesse's reception in America is quite different from that of his reception in Germany. Although several of his works had appeared in translation throughout the years, he was all but unknown in this country when he received the Nobel Prize for Literature in 1946. The American press for the most part ignored him, even when he received this prestigious award. It was only in the late 1950s that Americans began to become interested in his work. Today, of course, he has become a cult figure. Hesse is without doubt one of the very favorite authors of college-age Americans. Similarly, most of the serious scholarly criticism on Hesse in recent years has been written in English, and most of the important books have been written by North Americans.

It is certainly easy to see why American youth is interested in Hesse. The problems with which he deals in his stories and novels have meaning for young people in this country today. His treatment of adolescence, the problems of growing up, authority, rebellion, the "establishment," sex, human relationships, and, to a lesser extent, drugs, is significant and "relevant." Likewise, many young people share Hesse's interest in Oriental philosophy and in a non-dogmatic theology. It must, however, be pointed out that many important elements of Hesse's thought are overlooked by the majority of his admirers. For example, one often sees a devotion to self-discipline and hard work directed toward the achievement of some specific goal in Hesse's work. Especially Demian, Siddhartha, and Joseph Knecht attain a remarkable amount of self-discipline while still quite young, and it becomes clear in the respective works that the success and happiness of these characters is possible only because of their earlier rigorous training. If Hesse does not share the Protestant ethic of hard work, he nonetheless sees and portrays in his novels the necessity of building one's life on a firm foundation. Many of his works also show the other side of the coin - the results of not building one's life on a firm foundation (e.g., Klein and Knulp, who is much less happy than the more disciplined wanderer Goldmund). Hesse in no way respects bourgeois narrow-mindedness, complacency, and resistance to change at all cost; but neither does he express approval of destructive rebellion for its own sake. The freedom of Hesse's characters is a reflection of a successful, integrated life; they are slaves neither to tradition nor to their own weaknesses.

It is especially ironic that Hesse has become a folk hero and a model for an entire generation, for Hesse's most important **theme** throughout his mature works is the necessity of each individual finding his own way in life, rather than following the doctrine or teachings of an authority-figure, however noble or admirable such a figure may be. Often the incidentals of Hesse's novels and stories-rebellion against authority, sexual freedom, etc. - are religiously praised and faithfully followed by his young readers, who thereby completely lose touch with the fundamental aspect of Hesse's thought: the value of an individual's determining, choosing, and continually reexamining his own values. Surely nothing is more foreign to Hesse than the idea that "I have found the way, and there is no other." And this is indeed the narrow-minded philosophy of some of those who have chosen Hesse as their hero and mentor.

It is difficult to predict what direction Hesse's future popularity will take. More and more of his works are being translated into English - short stories, essays on various subjects, poems, autobiographical sketches, indeed almost anything will be eagerly purchased by his faithful reading public. Sooner or later a reaction must take place. Much of Hesse's short prose fiction is not especially rich or rewarding; his essays are to a great extent dated and have only historical interest; his range as a poet is narrow and poetry is in any event difficult to translate, or to appreciate in translation; and his autobiographical works are unquestionably among his least successful. It is to be hoped that these minor works will enable the American reader to more fully appreciate the complexity of Hesse, without detracting from his truly great novels and short stories.

# NARCISSUS AND GOLDMUND

## INTRODUCTION

### NOTE TO THE STUDENT

This study-guide is intended to aid you in your evaluation and appreciation of Hesse's *Narcissus and Goldmund*. All other works of Hesse that are referred to are analyzed strictly for the light they throw on the central work under discussion. Most of this study-guide will make sense to you only if you are already familiar with at least *Narcissus and Goldmund* in either English translation or German original. The basic assumption throughout this discussion is that it will prompt you to refer back to your original text.

-The Editors

### THEMES, MOTIFS, AND STYLE IN NARCISSUS AND GOLDMUND

#### Life as Tension and Attraction between Antithetical Forces

The individual is caught in this polarity but cognizance of one's own type can provide direction. Thus the introvert

Narcissus lives in accordance with the demands of his 'type,' the extravert Goldmund in line with the dictates of his personality. Nonetheless, the opposing forces remain operative within the individual. Narcissus is forever attracted to Goldmund, as Goldmund is forever fascinated with the world of Narcissus. The names 'Narcissus' and 'Goldmund' mirror this mutual attraction of polar opposites. Narcissus, in line with the mythological youth who fell in love with his own reflection in the water, is reflective, self-contained, and introspective. He dreams of boys, as he puts it. But his name also suggests what attracts him to Goldmund. It connotes beauty and thus evokes a central characteristic of Goldmund. The name Goldmund, on the other hand, not only evokes Goldmund's nature as a lover, in that he has a golden mouth for courting and kissing, but suggests a trait Goldmund admires in Narcissus. It suggests articulateness, golden words which Narcissus possesses to a far greater degree than Goldmund.

## Friendship

Although there are erotic overtones in the relationship between Narcissus and Goldmund, their fascination is for the opposite they sense in each other. Their friendship gives much strength to both Narcissus and Goldmund. It is connected with the **theme** of Permanence and Union in that their friendship is manifest throughout the novel.

## The Outsider

Being extreme types, both Narcissus and Goldmund are loners. Though they may be highly successful in their chosen way of life, they are not 'social animals.' The benefits of 'belonging' are reserved for people like the Abbot Daniel, whose personality fuses features of both Goldmund and Narcissus.

## Mind versus Senses

The two friends are not only psychological opposites (extravert vs. introvert), but intellectual opposites as well. Narcissus is the thinker, he is cool, disciplined, analytical, abstract. Goldmund is warmhearted and hotblooded. He does not think abstractly, but in images. He proceeds intuitively and is a creature of moods. Above all, he is a lover.

## Art as a Mediator

Art provides esthetic form to raw life. The subject the artist takes from real life is thus transformed. It no longer is transient, but as art it is permanent. Artistic form is a product of the creative mind. It expresses man's antipathy for the transient and chaotic in life. The idea of permanence, however, if it is not incorporated in an object perceived through the senses as real, is an empty notion. Thus in art the ideal and real meet; the notion of permanence becomes physical reality, the stuff of transient reality becomes permanent.

## Permanence versus Transience

Transience characterizes the world of the senses. The most intense form of sensuality, love-making, demonstrates the innate brevity of sense experience. Goldmund's life is suffused with the realization of transitoriness. Nothing lasts for him. He has scores of affairs and he cannot abide permanent relationships save his friendship with Narcissus. In contrast, Narcissus' life spells permanence. The cloister, which has been there forever, is his habitat. Narcissus' life in it is without significant fluctuation.

## Recurrence

The **theme** of recurrence has a mediating function between permanence and transience. Mariabronn, it seems, has been there since time immemorial, yet forever new generations of students pass through its portals. Events in Goldmund's life also recur, above all his love-making. He returns to Master Niklaus' city, the castle, the cloister, and as Theodore Ziolkowski points out, "a very strong seasonal movement carries the narrative along."

## Love and Death

Goldmund experiences that love and death, and life and death are two sides of the same coin. The innate brevity of love-making, and all sensual experience brings on the consciousness of the passage of time. And at the end of time, there is death. The proximity of love and life on one hand, and death on the other is echoed time and again in the novel. For example, Goldmund as the lover of Agnes almost loses his life; people, moribund with the plague seek relief in orgies.

## The Great Mother

The Great Mother symbolically encompasses life and death. She gives Goldmund's life direction and fulfillment. (The Great Mother archetype is discussed extensively in the chapter on Influences And Formal Aspects and also in the chapter on Textual Analysis.)

## The Father

Negatively, the symbol of the Father stands for restriction and domination, exemplified especially by Goldmund's own father, and positively, for order and knowledge as represented primarily by Narcissus.

## The Horse

According to Cirlot's Dictionary of Symbols, among other connotations the horse has a Jungian meaning. This seems to be the most probable one in *Narcissus and Goldmund*, where the horse would be an adjunct symbol of the Great Mother. Goldmund's relationship with his horse Bless is of great intimacy; Bless might be a surrogate for his forgotten mother. The horse is also connected with Agnes, the most formidable Mother figure Goldmund knows, and also with Lydia. Though she caused Goldmund to be ejected from the castle she once more returns to her role as Goldmund's would-be lover when she sends him some tokens of her love. Her emissary uses a horse to bring them to him. Out in the wintry world, Goldmund wants and needs this horse quite badly. He thinks of committing murder to get it. Significantly, as the knight leads him out of the 'Father World' of the castle, he uses no horse, but takes Goldmund the long distance they travel on foot.

## The Dog

According to Cirlot, the dog is related to Mother symbolism, to death and resurrection. Goldmund faints while looking at the dog heads carved in the arch under which he stands. Upon awakening, he thinks of them once again. The occasion of his fainting releases his lost memories of his mother. This is the prerequisite event that enables him to escape the confining world of the cloister and, in a sense, to be resurrected to his true being as a creature of the Mother World.

## Water

Water is Hesse's favorite symbol. In *Narcissus and Goldmund* it has baptismal and initiating functions and qualities at the threshold of new phases in Goldmund's life. As the river it signals to Goldmund the alluring mysteries of transitoriness.

## Setting

The novel is set in the Middle Ages in what might be the Rhenish region of Germany; the city of Master Niklaus might be Cologne. However the exact time and places are not specified, although the plague and the pogroms of the Jews suggest the fourteenth century. Hesse is deliberate in not being narrowly historical. He wishes to create an aura of timelessness, structurally an antipode to the notion of transience. Theodore Ziolkowski lists an impressive array of medieval literature Hesse knew, from the chivalric **epics** and the Minnesingers to Dante. He also was familiar with historical studies on the age, on monastic life in medieval Germany, and on medieval wood carving. But Hesse does not deposit his specialized knowledge in a realist's fashion in *Narcissus and Goldmund.* There is little detail about the world of physical objects and processes, such as Master Niklaus' studio, or the art of wood carving. If Hesse wants the reader to see this world, it is with his mind's eye. The external, physical world is symbolic; it evokes another level of reality. For example, Goldmund's love-making is never depicted in differentiated clarity. All that Hesse says in effect is that Goldmund loves each girl differently and well. What emerges very clearly, however, is that all of Goldmund's women merge into the Great Mother image. Likewise, Hesse is not at all interested in the Middle Ages as history per se. There is not "a spark of genuine piety in Hesse's medieval world," as one critic has observed. The setting of *Narcissus and Goldmund* is not objective, external and realistic. It is symbolic; it is the landscape of the soul.

## Style

Hesse's style would likewise have to be described as symbolic. Although actual events are important, although they clearly mark the plotlines, every important detail in the novel points beyond itself to a fictive meaning dictated by the thematic structure of the book. The spirit is Narcissus' domain. The cloister's function is to symbolize it. The realm of ideas is the true dimension of reality for him. Goldmund's existence, too, is in the final analysis aligned with an 'idea.' Goldmund's images are accorded the rank of true ideas by Narcissus.

In the stricter sense, the style of *Narcissus and Goldmund* has to be defined as lyrical. By Hesse's own admission, he is not a novelist in the vein of Turgenev, Dickens, and Keller. He resembles rather the romantic writer Eichendorff, who ostensibly wrote novellas in which lyric poetry was disguised as prose. As Hesse himself observed: "The story as masked lyric poetry, the novel as a label borrowed for the attempts of poetic personalities to express their experience of themselves and the world, this was specifically a German and Romantic matter, in this I realized I was involved and I share the responsibility." This hybrid quality that seems somewhat illegitimate to Hesse and to some of his critics explains much of the magic of Hesse's style.

To the contemporary reader the integrity of the literary **genre** is no longer of great importance. Each work of art, he feels, is an autonomous creation and therefore must be judged on its own terms. In Hesse's time, however, the tradition to be emulated by the novelist was that of the great realists of the nineteenth century, not the romantics who frequently fused the **genres** and who often produced weak novels.

Hesse's **syntax** is parataxis. It tends to avoid subordinating conjunctions and clauses which would allow for the precise differentiations necessary for complex thought. As a result, Hesse's style is not analytical, but evocative; it appeals to the reader's emotive, not his cerebral faculties. Technically speaking - the original German must be used here as an example - Hesse uses the following devices of lyrical form:

1. **Alliteration** 2. Repetition 3. Rhythm:

Schau, bald holt auch uns der Tod, und wir verfaulen im Feld, mit unseren Knochen wurfelt der Maulwurf. Lass uns vorher noch leben und lieb miteinander sein.

These, as a great many lines in *Narcissus and Goldmund*, could easily be rearranged in terms of a poem. There is a profusion of 'l,' 't' (final d equals t in German), and 'f' sounds. The syllable 'ver' is complemented by 'Feld' (v equals f in German), and 'wurf(elt)' is echoed by '(Maul) wurf.' The rhythm is lyrical, i.e., syntactic segments are duplicated with a recognizable regularity.

## Sense Appeal

The lyrical quality of Hesse's style in *Narcissus and Goldmund* makes for a blending of the sensory data transmitted to the reader so that no single sense prevails or is dominant.

## Narrative Point of View

The point of view is basically that of the omniscient narrator. There is some dialogue, however, and especially conversations between Narcissus and Goldmund are highly revealing. Dialogue is Hesse's main device for letting Narcissus and Goldmund come to life as characters. In their tension-charged exchanges can be recognized two definite human egos in the dialectic of self-assertion. Even when Goldmund has accepted the loss of self in the end, his very denial of the ego challenges Narcissus.

The omniscient stance allows the narrator to move his characters precisely along the lines he intends to develop in his novel. They do not get away from him. By speaking for Goldmund as well as for Narcissus, he can stress and reveal with some objectivity their typological characteristics. But there are drawbacks to the omniscient narrator frame; they are noticeable quite plainly in Narcissus and Goldmund. We have the feeling that we see only very small portions of the protagonists' minds, and those often hazily. Thorough empathy with them is therefore out of the question. But this in another perspective is an asset. Hesse's approach in Narcissus and Goldmund makes for what might be called 'objectified empathy.' For example, the narrator tells us about Goldmund's moods and perceptions, some of which are startlingly consonant with feelings about and insights into life we ourselves have experienced. Experience, then, in *Narcissus and Goldmund,* often has an air of universal validity.

## Humor

There is virtually no humor in *Narcissus and Goldmund*. In the earlier *Steppenwolf* humor had played a central role, both as therapy for Haller advocated by the immortals, and as **irony**, a stylistic feature. The absence of humor in *Narcissus and Goldmund*, especially in the middle section of the novel that has Goldmund go through his often preposterous antics, may account in part for the reservations some critics have about the book. If the balances which Hesse asserted to be equal for both **protagonists** are in fact too heavily in Goldmund's favor, a humorous or ironic slant on Goldmund's escapades might have lightened him a bit.

## The Translation

The translation that is most readily available is by Ursule Molinaro. It deserves high praise. Though felicitous, it hardens somewhat the mellifluence of Hesse's style. An exact transcription of Hesse's German would have to be considered 'mushy' in English. Molinaro's attitude toward Hesse's style seems, to this reader, to be not without some ironic reservations. For example, the German word 'ach,' with all its sentimental **connotations** of "Weltschmerz," is left untranslated beginning about three fourths through the book.

# NARCISSUS AND GOLDMUND

## TEXTUAL ANALYSIS

### CHAPTER ONE

........................................................

**Exposition.** The main task facing an author during the initial phases of writing a drama or novel is not only to introduce the characters and to show their background, but also to identify or suggest the central problems of the work.

Figurative Anticipation. The literary artist will often attempt to influence the reader by subtle devices so that he is unconsciously sympathetic to the writer's artistic aims. The writer, in other words, programs the reader in the introductory passages of the work so that he will follow the story in the firm belief that the events in it must come about by some law of necessity. Especially in the first chapter of *Narcissus and Goldmund,* Hesse makes use of such anticipatory devices. In subtle lines he draws a preliminary sketch of the large plot patterns and themes.

The Journey. The big chestnut tree in front of the cloister had come from Italy. A monk who had left the cloister for a pilgrimage to Rome had brought it back with him. Here the motif of travel is introduced; it prefigures Goldmund's pattern of travel away from and back to Mariabronn. Goldmund, too, leaves a symbol of his wanderings to the cloister. From his pilgrimage through the world, he brings back the knowledge of wood carving which enables him to sculpture a magnificent work of art for the cloister.

Transitoriness and Recurrence. Generation after generation of school boys pass by the chestnut tree. They all resemble one another, though, of course, they are always different. Here Hesse introduces the motif of transience and the notion of recurrence. Most of Goldmund's experiences are succinctly characterized by their brevity and transience, above all his endless succession of love affairs. They strike the reader largely as phenomena of recurrence.

Dichotomy and Union. The novel has as **protagonists** two men who are complete opposites in character. Neither of them can ever be like the other. Because of and in spite of this, they admire, even love one another. But their love unites them only in a figurative sense. They are called "lost halves of one another." Together they would form a complete whole, a harmonious, in fact, an ideal human being. The notion of contrast and union is introduced early in the chapter. The cloister, embracing and harmonizing all activities within it, is described in a long series of contrasts. In Mariabronn there is teaching and studying, the arts and sciences, piety and worldliness, the frivolous and somber, simplicity and cunning. Faith is promoted in the cloister, credulity smiled upon.

The relationship of *Narcissus and Goldmund* is prefigured in terms of both dichotomy and union. Before Goldmund is introduced to the story, we meet Narcissus and the Abbot Daniel.

The Abbot is not a scholar but a man of feeling who thinks in images. But he is also a manager; he is dedicated to service and holds the position to which Narcissus aspires. Therefore he is not only a foil for Goldmund, but for Narcissus as well. The Abbot Daniel thus represents a fusion of *Narcissus and Goldmund*. He is dedicated to order, but not coldly and analytically like Narcissus. His orientation in life is emotional, like Goldmund's.

The dichotomy of Narcissus and Goldmund is fated and eternal. It sets them apart from everyone else since the concept of union is applicable only to lesser people. The Abbot symbolizes that union. He is a harmonious person, but Hesse signals that he is not of the same caliber as either Narcissus or Goldmund. In his perceptivity the Abbot is, in fact, rather limited. When he asks Narcissus to reveal to him what the future holds, the analytical Narcissus by logical inference simply extends the known lines of the Abbot's life pattern into the future. Abbot Daniel, however, calls him a mystic and a romantic, a man who has visions. He does so because he himself can think only in images.

The Outsider. Upon his arrival at the cloister, the boy Goldmund immediately becomes aware of his status as an outsider. He is treated like one by the rest of the boys who ridicule him for having fallen asleep in class. Essentially, being an outsider is a condition Goldmund cannot escape for the rest of his life. Narcissus shares this fate. Although he is very much a member of the cloister, he is not popular. He is a loner because of his intelligence and arrogance. But Narcissus is not an outsider in the strict sense of the word; he does not reject the social order, but works within it.

The Lover. As Goldmund sits through his first lesson he watches his handsome and excellent teacher Narcissus and immediately likes him. This feeling for Narcissus gratifies and relaxes Goldmund so that feeling very secure, he falls asleep in class. Although other boys tease him for it and call him a baby, the word is not meant altogether in derision. His classmates, paradoxically, since Goldmund is an outsider, take a liking to him almost immediately, even though Goldmund fights with one of them for being teased. Goldmund is, of course, a person of extraordinary attractiveness. He is a lover. In some form or other, love is rarely denied him.

Learning and Character Development. Goldmund is ignorant when he enters the cloister. He does not know what is going on in class. Because he is unaware of the rules that govern life at school, he gets into trouble. But he is intelligent; he recognizes that his fighting with his classmate was ill-mannered and foolish and consequently, he makes peace. Goldmund's story can be told in terms of a learning about life. He is aided in his endeavor by prodigious gifts, an unquenchable thirst for experience and great faculties of intuitive insight.

# NARCISSUS AND GOLDMUND

## TEXTUAL ANALYSIS

### CHAPTER TWO

The Father and the Mother Worlds. The two worlds are first alluded to openly in this chapter. Goldmund's mother, we learn later in the novel, was an extremely sensual, wild, and adventurous woman who abandoned her husband and baby son. Goldmund's father succeeded in erasing nearly all of his son's memories of his mother and wishes to conclude his efforts by ordaining a life in the cloister for Goldmund. There, in the realm of academic learning and service, of thinking and order, the father feels the boy will be rescued forever from the world of the Mother. Although Goldmund's memories of his mother are blocked, he longs for her world. We see this in his love and admiration for the Abbot Daniel. The Abbot, who shares some basic character traits with Goldmund, must be seen at least to some degree as a resident of the Mother World. Thus he is the natural object of love while Goldmund is still unaware of his own type. Once Narcissus is able to awaken Goldmund to the knowledge of his mother, he will no longer be torn between the Abbot and Narcissus. He will no longer need the Abbot. Through

Narcissus' direction he will know that he belongs to the world of the Mother and that he must find fulfillment in it to find himself. But while Goldmund is still unaware of the Mother World he wishes to find fulfillment in the world of the Father.

Narcissus as the Object of Goldmund's Love. The Father World is represented above all by Narcissus. Goldmund's own father is a negative representative of this world in that, unlike Narcissus, he is inimical towards the Mother World. Consequently, Goldmund has no love for him. Goldmund's love focuses on Narcissus because he senses his opposite in him and because Narcissus, at the same time, is not at all antagonistic towards the Mother World.

Goldmund as the Object of Narcissus' Love. Narcissus and Goldmund are different in quality from all other figures in the novel because of their "obvious gifts, both had the mark of fate." Goldmund is the prototype of the world of the Mother, of feeling and the sensual life. Narcissus is fully conscious of lacking all the qualities Goldmund has in abundance. Being a highly aloof person, he lives life vicariously, above all through Goldmund who has such prodigious gifts for living. Narcissus, we may say, loves himself in Goldmund by seeing him as his lost half and surrogate self.

The Incipience of the Quest for the Self. Even before Narcissus awakens Goldmund to the knowledge of belonging to the Mother World, Goldmund feels at times he does not belong in the cloister and has thoughts of running away. Narcissus, on the other hand, does not need to undergo a search for his goal, because his superior consciousness has already inferred it. Knowing his goal, Narcissus must maintain and assert the self to realize it; this process is not without suffering. Narcissus has to seek solitude to counteract the danger of losing the self. This explains his aloofness; Narcissus does not readily open himself up even to Goldmund. He despises the spectacle of the teacher who falls in love with a student and objects when Goldmund wishes to stroke his hair. Narcissus, though he is confined to the cloister, finds an outward fulfillment in a life of service. His professional development is an "outer" one; it is the external occurrence of something Narcissus anticipated in his mind. He is certain from the onset of all his gifts and his eventual position of leadership. There is no drifting in Narcissus' life; it follows a pattern fully visible to Narcissus from the beginning.

Goldmund's road to fulfillment is "inward." Through all his peregrinations, his search is for the Great Mother in his own soul. His quest is for the knowledge through experience that he belongs to the world of the Mother. In contrast to Narcissus, he must learn to lose the self to realize this goal.

Goldmund's Foray into the Village. Goldmund's nocturnal excursion into the village precipitates and anticipates his departure from Mariabronn into the world. The **episode** has the further structural function of trying together the beginning and the end of the novel. In the end, Goldmund makes another excursion into the world. There he is initiated into death when the Great Mother takes his heart out. Here at the beginning of the book, Goldmund is initiated into life when the kiss he receives from the girl in the village awakens his senses. His conviction of belonging in the cloister is greatly shaken. After returning to Mariabronn, Goldmund weeps and is comforted by Narcissus. Now when Goldmund slips over into the world of feeling, he can be a more meaningful friend to Narcissus, to whom a Goldmund oriented in feeling is a more authentic person. Typically aloof, Narcissus is reticent in expressing his emotions directly and resorts to the Latin amicus meus to indicate to Goldmund that he considers him a friend.

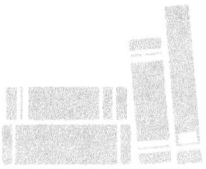

# NARCISSUS AND GOLDMUND

## TEXTUAL ANALYSIS

### CHAPTER THREE

Love and Confusion. As a dutiful cloister student, Goldmund feels that his attraction for the sensual must not be directed at the girl he kissed. Not yet knowing that he has no business being at Mariabronn, he also focuses the sensual component of love on Narcissus. He wishes to make this possible by "spiritualization" of "the flames" of the senses. What Goldmund seems to have in mind is some form of spiritual consummation of his love for his friend. Narcissus perceives Goldmund's confusion and wishes to persuade him that they are two halves irretrievably lost to each other. There is a spiritual attraction for one another, but there can be no consummation of their love. Narcissus understands Goldmund's confusion; he is also able to uncover the reason for Goldmund's rejection of the lure of the Mother World. Goldmund's father is the culprit. He turned the child against love and emotion, thus against sex and the Mother World. Narcissus draws this conclusion when he observes that Goldmund cannot evoke any images in the listener when he talks about his father. Goldmund indicts his father, so to speak, by thinking about him in "appropriate" terms. The suggestion is that Goldmund's father cannot appear in image thinking because it is the type of thought characteristic of the Mother World, which Goldmund's father rejects. Despite his confusion over his unclear relationship with Narcissus, Goldmund continues to grow away from the cloister. He develops, for example, preferences for aspects of monastic life that suggest some of the concerns and goals of his future life. He loves to sing in the student choir and favors hymns in honor of the Virgin Mary; he roams the countryside and goes hunting and he also enjoys listening to the Mass (the liturgy, full of archetypal content, appeals to the soul and the senses, not to the mind). Most importantly, Goldmund feels drawn to the art objects in the cloister. As the artist-to-be, he senses their special relationship to him.

# NARCISSUS AND GOLDMUND

## TEXTUAL ANALYSIS

### CHAPTER FOUR

Clearing up the Confusion. The content and purpose of the dialogue between Narcissus and Goldmund is dictated by Narcissus who wishes to make Goldmund see that they can never truly come together as friends, that they are radically different types. In order to convince him, Narcissus has to maneuver Goldmund into remembering his mother, for then Goldmund will have found the object with which, figuratively speaking, he can consummate his love. He will be ready then to reject the cloister, the Father World, and the notion that he and Narcissus can stay together; he can go in search of sensual experience. Goldmund will no longer be confused.

This dialogue can be of greater effectiveness than those of the past because the two friends have developed a language that is more suitable than that of logic and reason. "A language of the soul and of signs had gradually developed between them.... Gradually, the imaginative power of Goldmund's soul had found its way into Narcissus' thought and language." Narcissus, in turn, had learned to understand much in Goldmund's nature and his feelings.

Perspective of Differentiation. Narcissus asserts that he, in contrast to Goldmund, is a man of science. He is analytical; he establishes differentiations between phenomena.

Perspective of Union. Goldmund denies that it is essential to dwell on differences. It is child's play and to Goldmund indicates intellectual arrogance. Goldmund stresses the importance of similarities. All men are united by the same destiny that intends them to find eternal bliss in God

Perspective of Differentiation. To Narcissus, man's destiny is a personal matter. Dogma, in view of which everyone is meant to do and to be the same, is not life. In life people are as different as Judas who betrayed Christ and John who stayed by his side to the end.

Goldmund's Rebuttal. Goldmund calls Narcissus a sophist, implying that Narcissus above all else wants to win the argument, even if it involves statements Narcissus does not really believe in. Goldmund is justified in accusing Narcissus of sophistry because Narcissus as a Christian should accept dogma. However, Narcissus has other priorities; Goldmund's self-realization is more important to him than articles of faith.

Perspective of Differentiation. Narcissus accepts Goldmund's rebuttal. Instead of pursuing the argument in terms that seem intellectual games to Goldmund, he tailors his points to concepts more attuned to Goldmund's thinking. Narcissus uses the language of **metaphor** to convince Goldmund. "It is not our task to come together, not any more than sun and moon or sea and land can come together. We, dear friend, are sun and moon....

Our goal is...not to merge with one another, but to recognize one another...as the other's opposite and complement."

Goldmund's Answer. There is no effective rebuttal by Goldmund, but he is sensitive to the fact that Narcissus is now arguing in a different key. Goldmund feels Narcissus talks down to him, as if he were a child and is angry that Narcissus does not take him seriously.

Conclusion. Narcissus wins this phase of the argument by exploiting Goldmund's answer. He insists that he takes him very seriously when he is Goldmund, but not when he fancies himself an intellectual. Goldmund, in other words, is his equal, child or not, if he simply lets himself become what he is meant to be. Goldmund, perplexed and hurt, ends the discussion.

The Dialogue Continued. Narcissus clearly dominates the second phase of the argument. He switches his premise, stressing the notion of union, and thereby gains a tremendous tactical advantage over Goldmund. He states that he wants to awaken Goldmund to self-recognition. He himself is highly conscious, Goldmund is less so. Thus there is differentiation only in degree. Narcissus assures him that he will be superior to Narcissus once he has become fully conscious. Goldmund's superiority will be that of experience.

Narcissus connects the notion of experience and consciousness in an ingenious fashion by telling Goldmund that the prerequisite for experience is the memory of his childhood. Goldmund's childhood implies consciousness of his mother. This in turn implies the world of sensual experience, ultimately a consciousness of self for Goldmund, since Goldmund's self is to be realized in experience. Narcissus' demand for a remembered childhood is traumatic for Goldmund. He feels as though Narcissus had "plunged a knife into him."

Although it seems that Narcissus is coldly trapping Goldmund by his logic, there is intense intoxication in his rhetoric. He does speak the language of the soul when he once again states the differences between them. They are fundamental but they do not spell inequality. "Your origin is from the Mother. You were given the strength to love and to live. We creatures of the mind...live in an arid realm.... Your home is the earth, ours the mind. Your danger is drowning in the sensual world, ours is suffocation in an airless void. You are an artist, I am a thinker. You sleep at the breast of the Mother, I wake in the desert." Narcissus, in fact, does not persuade Goldmund so much as he awakens him.

The dialogue has undergone a metamorphosis in form. It began as a philosophical discussion of friendship and in the end is a test of strength, an act of rivalry. Narcissus began by stressing the differences between them but elicited from Goldmund only an insistence on their friendship. He switched to the notion of union and finally succeeded in forcing Goldmund to see their friendship as competition. The dialogue began on an academic and ends on an existential note. For all the indications to the contrary, Narcissus has not tricked Goldmund. It was Goldmund who chose the weapons; whereas Narcissus wished to weigh ideas and to argue by logic, Goldmund opted for a battle of personalities.

The Awakening. Goldmund awakens in more than a figurative sense. He had fainted as a result of the anguish Narcissus' words had caused him. When he gains consciousness, he has recollections of a number of dazzling dream images central to which, he realizes, is the image of his mother. "Like a warm wind her image floated through him, like a cloud of warmth and tenderness and intimate enticement. Oh, mother. Oh, how was it possible, how could I have forgotten you."

Now that Goldmund has remembered his mother, it will only be a question of time until he will accept the implications. He will enter on a search for her, a search that is symbolic for a journey into the Mother World, the life of sensual experience.

# NARCISSUS AND GOLDMUND

## TEXTUAL ANALYSIS

### CHAPTER FIVE

Leave Taking. Goldmund's mother, whom he resembles closely, had been a person unsuited to domestication. She had strayed from home for days and weeks at a time and had finally disappeared forever. This pattern, evoking the **theme** of the journey, outlines Goldmund's behavior during his final period at Mariabronn. He, too, leaves the "nest" temporarily for rides and walks and in the end he breaks away from the cloister altogether.

Dichotomy and Union in a New Key. Upon remembering his mother, Goldmund is dumbfounded by the realization that he could ever have forgotten her. Never in his life had he loved anyone as much. He had "venerated" and "admired" her; she was "sun" and "moon" to him. Significantly, as Goldmund's quest for self-realization begins, the images of sun and moon are repeated here. Narcissus had used them to impress upon Goldmund that the two friends were fated to be different, that they were not meant to come together. Goldmund's mother is both sun and moon to him. She is the manifestation of the archetype of the

Great Mother in Goldmund's early life and as a symbol of union, she foreshadows the goal and success of Goldmund's quest. It is the search for the Great Mother by which he will find self-realization.

Parallelism and Contrast. As Goldmund takes a significant step forward in awareness of himself and his destiny, Narcissus' life changes also. He completes his novitiate and becomes a monk. Narcissus feels the need for seclusion, for long prayers, and for voluntary penance. As Goldmund is about to embark on a life of self-gratification, Narcissus embarks upon a life of self-discipline.

The Soul Comes Alive. In a sense, Goldmund, even before the actual occasion for leaving the cloister arises, no longer belongs at Mariabronn. He dreams luxurious dreams about a darkly sensual and fascinating existence in the Mother World. It would look upon him "from mysterious eyes of love," utter "caressing" sounds of "endearment," engulf him in "sweetness" and touch him with "silken hair."

His breaking away from the Father World is not without feelings of guilt. In his dreams the Virgin, his mother, and a lover fuse into one; he feels these dreams are unpardonable, horrendous crimes and sins. He dreams of being in water; fish swim towards and through him. Here Goldmund's oneness with the Mother World, which water symbolizes, is established. His dreams also contain symbols of creativity. He sees himself as forming little clay figures to whom he gives huge genitals. They come to life, grow to giant proportions and move past him into the world.

The world of his soul is now more real to him than the activities of the cloister. After having repressed his Mother images for so long, they now flood his consciousness. They affect and transform even things that have the unequivocal properties of the world of the mind. Letters change into the scented face of his mother. Or they become a running horse, or a snake that moves through flowers. It seems at first incongruous that all this should happen in the cloister, the supreme symbol of the spirit in the novel. But the Mother World is larger than any province of the Father World. The cloister is thus full of infusions from the Mother World such as the chestnut tree and the cult of Mary. Goldmund returns to it definitely as a citizen of the Mother World. The name of the cloister, after all, is Mariabronn (fountain of Mary) and highly suggestive of the Mother World.

Goldmund Comes into His Own. Goldmund finally concedes that he was not meant to be a scholar. For scientists, letters do not and must not change into birds and serpents, Narcissus tells him. Science deals with the real, not the possible. The mind does not live in nature, but against it. Goldmund is now inclined to think of matters of the mind in negative terms, as "father things" and as "mother-hostile." Though he is somewhat contemptuous of the mind, he still hesitates to make a decision against becoming a monk. Of course, such a decision would be tantamount to leaving Narcissus. Again Narcissus steers him. He asks if Goldmund wants to go back to his father, intimating that Goldmund should go somewhere. Goldmund instantly knows that he will not return to his father but also understands what Narcissus is really suggesting. His stay at Mariabronn is terminal. Narcissus clarifies for Goldmund what this realization means with regard to their friendship. It has reached its goal. Goldmund has become aware.

Since Goldmund has accepted himself as Narcissus' opposite, Narcissus can intimate Goldmund's road ahead by sketching his own future as a contrast. Narcissus' path is to stay in the cloister, to be a monk, to fast and to exercise. He will be novice-master and Abbot, perhaps even bishop someday. He will live a life of service. By implication, Goldmund's life will have to be one of abandonment to the senses, a life of gratification of the appetites. He will roam far and wide into the world.

Knowing what his life shall be, Goldmund decides to leave the cloister. Again Narcissus steers Goldmund by example. He disappears into seclusion. Goldmund takes leave from the few people and especially the things he likes at the cloister. Among them the works of art have become most dear to him.

# NARCISSUS AND GOLDMUND

## TEXTUAL ANALYSIS

### CHAPTER SIX

........................................................................

Departure. Goldmund's final departure from Mariabronn is prefaced by a short, but significant absence from it. He is sent on a mission of collecting herbs for medicinal purposes. In nature, Hesse suggests, Goldmund will find the therapy he needs. As he gathers his herbs, Goldmund feels entirely at home in nature and at peace with it. It exercises a spell over him, the effects of which are wonder and enchantment. Significantly, Goldmund falls asleep. But this awakening, unlike that of the first day in class, is not traumatic. It is not a fight that ensues, but love-making. Hesse uses the nature sleep as a topos familiar in German literature especially through Goethe's *Faust*. After having caused several deaths, Faust sleeps in nature to awaken as a reborn man detached from his past. Goldmund, too, is "reborn," born unto himself, as it were, for his sensual nature is set free in the arms of the gypsy girl, Lise, who teaches him to know love. In contrast to his studies at the cloister, Goldmund here is a student of enormous talent.

Separation and Bonds. Goldmund returns to Mariabronn to talk to Narcissus and to say good-by. As Goldmund is "wide awake" at this moment, conscious in the world of love, he finds Narcissus in the penitent's cell, looking like a corpse. Narcissus has to force himself to be attentive to Goldmund, so deep had he sunk into contemplation. Yet he understands fully the catalytic nature of Goldmund's experience and tells Goldmund he must leave the cloister. He knows Goldmund has "fallen in love." To Goldmund the experience is a call from his mother, to lead him "home." Goldmund senses that his love experience with Lise initiates a pattern, the purpose of which is to find himself through the image of the Great Mother. He reveals himself as a masterful student, for in this sphere he is as conscious as Narcissus is in his. The friends now part company. The dichotomy assumes a spatial sense, but there is also a strong restatement of the concept of union. Talking in the cell, they sit shoulder to shoulder, sad and yet happy in their "indestructible friendship."

Baptism. As Goldmund leaves Mariabronn he undresses to wade through the brook by the cloister and is thus "initiated" into life. When he had gone to the village on his foray with the boys, he had been able to cross the brook on a plank. This time there is no plank and no bridge. But even the plank had been wet, for crossing the brook the first time had been a sort of pre-initiation. Water **imagery** is abundant in *Narcissus and Goldmund.* Repeatedly, it signals the introduction into a different phase of Goldmund's life. Water also symbolizes recurrence; the crossing of the brook is repeated by Goldmund. But water also signals transience. In a stream, it moves constantly, is always different, yet always the same.

In leaving the cloister, Goldmund leaves an entire world. As he meets Lise amidst the enigmatic and alluring sounds of the night forest, he realizes the change. He calls for Lise with the cry of an owl. They meet but do not speak. They move like animals, searching for a spot to mate. In the cloister, speech, differentiated articulation, was demanded and in order. Here in the forest the demands of nature are understood and silently heeded.

# NARCISSUS AND GOLDMUND

## TEXTUAL ANALYSIS

### CHAPTER SEVEN

Patterns of Transformation. In addition to love-making, the experience with Lise teaches Goldmund that being away from the cloister is not equal to forgetting its principles and patterns. Up to now Goldmund had existed with other people in a social world. Although Narcissus had predicted that Goldmund would not stay with Lise, Goldmund has notions of living with her. But she surprises him by going back to her husband, although she knows he will beat her. Goldmund cannot hold her. He has to accept that the Goldmund who has become of age is confined as a wanderer to a form of existence that rules out social bonds. Although women strongly desire Goldmund as a lover, there is a basic difference between them and Goldmund. He yearns for the world of order and permanence, but he casts his lot with a free life. The women that love and leave him yearn for a free life, but cast their lot with their husbands and families, with order and security.

Goldmund feels stunned and abandoned by Lise's leaving him, but is able to fall asleep instantly, leaving his troubles behind. When he wakes up he is eager to learn to be a part of nature and to live off the land. Just as Lise abandoned him, he seems to be intent on abandoning the world of people. He wishes to "transform" himself into an animal. The chapter abounds with images of transformation. Goldmund sees a snake that turns out to be an empty skin. He thinks of being a bear loving a she-bear. He remembers earlier attempts at drawing in which the objects he sketched had a way of changing themselves into something else. Figures had turned into leaves; the mouth of a fish had become someone's eyebrow. He dreams he is a bear devouring Lise amidst caresses. These examples clearly demonstrate the undesirability and frightening excessiveness of Goldmund's notion of metamorphosis. The snake image showed its futility; the snake shed its skin, but remained what it was. Goldmund may live out in the wild, but he must remain a human being; for all his individuality, he needs human contact. He finally recognizes that living alone would be "unbearably sad"; not to make love again would be unthinkable.

Goldmund is eager for human companionship and happy to find it. He chances to come to a farm house where a little child plays in front of the door. But Goldmund is, of course, the outsider. Even the child senses it, for when Goldmund addresses him, the boy scurries off for the protection of the house. Goldmund is not meant to be a lasting part of a social environment such as a family. He oscillates between needing social contact and needing freedom, but in a rhythm favoring the latter.

The Outsider and the Lover. As the farmer returns from work, he finds Goldmund in his hut. Suspicious, he pulls him to the light to look him over. He laughs, giving Goldmund a well-meaning slap on the shoulder and invites him to eat with his family. But he rejects Goldmund's request for shelter, telling him to sleep outside. Goldmund is liked, yet he does not belong. The farmer's wife comes to love him in the night but returns to her husband like Lise.

Guilt. Goldmund finds that he has no feelings of guilt as an adulterer. While at Mariabronn he would rather have died than commit such a sin. Out in the open world he has a different sense of guilt. It is that of original sin which Goldmund connects with the sense of transitoriness. In terms of the Garden of Eden myth, the fruit of original sin is knowledge. The curse of knowledge is the consciousness of transience, i.e., of death. Out in the world, where Goldmund finds the joys of life, there is also the sadness of death. These feelings, expressed in this chapter in religious allusions, will converge more and more on the image of the Great Mother who encompasses both life and death.

# NARCISSUS AND GOLDMUND

## TEXTUAL ANALYSIS

## CHAPTER EIGHT

..................................................

Freedom and Domestication. This chapter explores the rhythm of oscillation between the life of freedom and the life of domesticity. The accent is definitely on the former. In the first half, we follow Goldmund as he roams the countryside unattached, a free spirit in one brief love encounter after another. He is superbly adept as a student of love. His experiences accumulate and classify themselves. He is able to give himself completely to every woman primarily because he is able to forget the last in the arms of the next. But he wonders why none of them wishes to share his life of wandering. Two answers occur to him. Is it, he muses, that women sense he is a wanderer and therefore will not cast their lot with him, or is it perhaps that he is simply desired as a pretty doll, to be hugged and thrown away. Both explanations are correct. Goldmund is fated to wander as a prerequisite for his self-realization. He is not domesticated and therefore his love-making is not routine. Love-making with Goldmund is, in fact, play; it is entirely free of responsibility. It is not a means to an end, and thus has no social bonding function.

Goldmund's life on the road oscillates into domestication when he spends a few months at a castle. Here special clothes are tailored for him which signal the two poles of freedom and domesticity within his nature. His outfit gives him the appearance half of a huntsman, half of a page. In the knight of the castle Goldmund finds a man whose background parallels his own. He also had been a scholar who had abandoned his studies for warfare and worldly affairs. Having made a pilgrimage to Rome and Constantinople, he now wishes to put down his memoirs. Goldmund is to help him in writing.

Though Goldmund now wanders only vicariously, i.e., along the paths of the knight's memory, he does not forsake his quest for love-making. The knight has two lovely daughters. Goldmund courts especially the older, Lydia. In time Lydia falls in love with Goldmund and brings herself to lying next to him in bed, but she refuses consummation. After several such frustrating experiences for Goldmund, the younger daughter, curious and jealous about the affair, joins them in bed. Here Goldmund learns that if given the choice between love and desire, he will opt for the latter. He turns to Julie and begins to make love to her hoping to go further with Julie than he had been able to with Lydia. Goldmund's love play is terminated by Lydia who then confesses all to her father.

To Goldmund, Lydia is the first woman he ever loved and who, he feels, has truly loved him. Goldmund then recognizes that love is more than desire, but nonetheless he chooses desire over love. For Lydia love is only possible in the confines of marriage. Without it, she feels her love for Goldmund is wrong. When Goldmund has made a choice for desire, he has in fact made a choice for the life on the open road and against domestication. He is ejected from the castle by the knight.

# NARCISSUS AND GOLDMUND

## TEXTUAL ANALYSIS

### CHAPTER NINE

The Road to Murder. Goldmund is turned out of the castle in the middle of winter; nonetheless a sense of freedom comes over him and he is ready to brave the hardships of the season. But he is not entirely without the comforts of the world he has just left. Sent by Lydia, the stableboy, Hans, comes riding after him to deliver a vest she had knitted for Goldmund, a gold piece and some ham. As Hans approaches as yet unrecognized, Goldmund thinks of murdering him to get the horse, but laughs about his fleeting intention when he recognizes Hans.

The thought of murder anticipates the dramatic focal point of the chapter, the murder of Viktor. Like Goldmund, Viktor is an escaped cloister student who looks half like a priest and half like a highway robber. In Viktor, Goldmund meets himself in his worst potential form and is alerted to some sad facts about his own life style. To be a lover one has to be young and handsome. With age comes ugliness and doors do not open readily. Then the wanderer has to think of nothing but survival. To succeed, he has to develop into a clever rapacious animal like Viktor who has consummate skill in detecting places to sleep and in smelling out houses where food can be found.

Goldmund reaches the low point of his journey when, being choked by Viktor who tries to steal his gold piece, he can survive only as a murderer. In murder Goldmund comes closest to a metamorphosis into an animal. The notion of transformation is again the signal that a period of domesticity lies ahead for Goldmund. Viktor's death is a figurative death for the totally shiftless Goldmund; but this "dying" involves deep agony. As he attempts to find a human settlement, he is half crazed by the trauma of murder, by hunger and cold. He insults the dead Viktor, jeering at him as if he were a fallen enemy. This is the behavior of primitive man. At this point Goldmund is furthest away from the world of Narcissus and it is no wonder that he insults him also. He implies that Narcissus is a coward who walls himself up against lurking death. All of Narcissus' fasting and praying won't keep death out, Goldmund jeers.

Goldmund has reached a point of deep despair. The world of freedom, the life on the road has revealed its dark and horrible side. The concept of love, too, is shown to have a dual face for when Goldmund reaches a human habitation he witnesses the birth of a child. The mother's pain and anguish produce a facial expression almost identical to that of the ecstasy of love.

In this pivotal chapter, Goldmund's quest for life has brought him to the edge of death and his search for love to the awareness of suffering. Death and suffering will be in the ascendency in Goldmund's life henceforth, though he will continue to find some happiness. But Goldmund will not face the next phase of his journey defenseless. He will discover a weapon by which death can be stalled and life be made "eternal." Goldmund discovers the world of art in the next phase of his domestication.

# NARCISSUS AND GOLDMUND

## TEXTUAL ANALYSIS

### CHAPTER TEN

The World of Art. The heavy use of the seasonal **imagery** of spring indicates that there is a new beginning in Goldmund's life. As he enters the world of Master Niklaus, he enters the atmosphere of the cloister all over again. On his way to Master Niklaus' city, however, he travels through a landscape very different from what he had so far encountered. No longer is it open country and forest with few settlements, primitive and backward in character. His journey now takes him through a densely populated region, through beautiful villages and prosperous towns. All these settlements suggest ordered societal existence, as did the cloister of Mariabronn.

Goldmund's experiences as he travels through this "cultural landscape," as the Germans call it, are duplications of those while at Mariabronn. He appears again as the Outsider and Lover. Goldmund observes a lovers' quarrel. When the man stalks off in a huff, Goldmund comforts and kisses the girl. But the man returns to the scene and a fight ensues. Goldmund wins the fight as he had the earlier one at Mariabronn, but there is a difference. At the cloister, he was welcomed into the group after the fight. Now Goldmund is totally the outsider. He fears reprisals and hurries away, continuing on his way half through the night before he goes to sleep. In a scene reminiscent of the Lise **episode**, he is awakened by a girl to whom he makes love. Then Goldmund finds shelter in a cloister, goes to mass and confession. But in contrast to his confession to Narcissus, he has now more on his conscience than having made love to a girl. Though the patterns of the past recur, it must be emphasized that Goldmund is no longer the innocent boy, but a man of experience. He is a murderer. On the other hand, the differences also convey an element of "sameness." Although Goldmund's "sin" is now of much greater magnitude, the priest is no more shocked about the murder than was Narcissus when Goldmund confessed to fornication.

The Revelation of Art. Goldmund sees a statue of Mary in a cloister which has a stunning effect on him. With the force of an epiphany, the world of art opens up to him. He learns that a certain Master Niklaus has created the madonna and decides to seek him out. He knows he wants to become an artist. Goldmund now has a goal definable in social terms. He is willing to commit himself to a long range purpose. He feels like a changed man in a changed world and hurries to the "bishop's city" where Master Niklaus lives. His plea for acceptance as a student contains a structural definition of art. Goldmund feels that in a work of art the detail corresponds in some subtle way to the whole, as the detail somehow also corresponds to other detail. But Goldmund is, of course, far from being primarily a theoretician of art. He proves he has the necessary practical gifts also. Asked to sketch something for the Master, he sets out to draw the head of Narcissus. The choice of Narcissus as Goldmund's first subject is not only based on Goldmund's love for his friend. Since Goldmund is in search of himself as part of the Mother World, one might expect him to draw the head of one of the women he loved. But as an initial venture, Narcissus is nonetheless the logical subject. Goldmund is a beginner and must learn the discipline, the control, the steadfast determination necessary to turn a mental picture into a crafted image. In other words, Goldmund's art at this stage needs Narcissus' world. Narcissus, then, who is the very embodiment of control and discipline, is a subject that by itself aids Goldmund in his task of convincing Master Niklaus that he can transform a mental picture into art. Later, when he is an accomplished artist, it will be Goldmund's highest aim to create an image of the Great Mother.

The Permanence of Art. As Goldmund waits for Master Niklaus to tell him whether or not he is accepted as an apprentice, he muses on the relationship between art and life. As we might expect, he perceives of it in terms of his own experiences. He has learned already to understand the transience of all human endeavors. Men, like water, must change and "trickle away." Art, in contrast, can survive the ages. Thus, he thinks, it is a bulwark against death, the fear of which to him seems perhaps to be the very root of art.

Art as a Way of Life. It would be in error to assume that art is the supreme goal of Goldmund's life. He does not complete his life on the note of artistic creation. Art cannot provide Goldmund with lasting satisfaction for to be fully committed to an artist's life he would have to turn into a societal creature. Already in this chapter there are indications of the damage that an artist's life inflicts on the person. Discipline and consistent work can diminish him. Deliberate to the point of pedantry, Master Niklaus, as far as Goldmund can tell, is not a happy man. Goldmund suffers tortures as Master Niklaus subjects him to a long wait before he tells him of his acceptance as an apprentice. When Goldmund is finally told, he gets very impatient because Master Niklaus cannot come to the point.

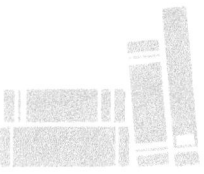

# NARCISSUS AND GOLDMUND

## TEXTUAL ANALYSIS

### CHAPTER ELEVEN

..................................................................

Contrary Forces in Balance; the Approximation of an Idyllic Life. While Goldmund is in the city, his life comes closest to being a happy one. There is the shelter the city can offer, yet there is also freedom for the pleasures of drinking and carousing, for gambling and brawling. Goldmund is even permitted to work irregular hours in Master Niklaus' shop. Nonetheless he imposes upon himself the discipline of sustained work on the statue of Narcissus. He names the statue St. John perhaps because in the church tradition St. John denotes chastity. In that sense, Goldmund confers a name on Narcissus that expresses a new and widened contrast between the friends. Goldmund is the man of experience, Narcissus the man of chastity. The contrast, of course, suggests also the notion of union in yearning. Experience is generally associated with the longing for innocence.

The forces of domestication and freedom can live side by side only because of Goldmund's commitment to the world of art. It is the great mediator. "Goldmund worked with deep love at the sculpture of Narcissus. In it he found himself, his artistry, and his soul every time he got off the track, which happened quite often." While Goldmund works, the awareness of the transient nature of all things and with it the consciousness of death is suspended. Here lies the ultimate meaning of artistic creation to Goldmund as a person.

But these moments of bliss are short. Goldmund has before him living proof that the rapture of artistic creativity offers no permanent happiness to the artist. In spite of being a very good artist, Master Niklaus is not joyful, not at peace with himself. Goldmund venerates but also hates him. The duality of attraction and repulsion exist with regard to Master Niklaus' daughter also. Lisbeth is beautiful and innocent, yet her innocence is not childlike, not human, in a sense. It seems incapable of ever being lost or of turning to pain and suffering. As perhaps a countermeasure to this orderly, even rigid and cold world of Master Niklaus' home, there grows in Goldmund the desire to create an image of the Great Mother someday. He has no idea about the details of the image, but only knows that it must express the "close relationship of ecstasy to pain and death."

Perhaps in order to assert the rights of this world that are totally absent in Master Niklaus' private life, Goldmund makes a small statue of Julie, the sensuous younger daughter of the knight. Master Niklaus, of course, disapproves of it; the statue is too unchaste for him. But Goldmund, by crafting it, has met the demands of the world of sensuality and is free to create St. John, the paragon of spirituality.

Maturity in Love. As Goldmund matures as an artist, he also matures as a man. He "had gradually lost the rest of his youthful grace and boyish innocence.... He had become a beautiful, strong man, much desired by women ..." Goldmund's love life consequently changes. His preference for young girls is tempered by the realization that older and less attractive women, too, have a special beauty unique to them in their love-making. In short, Goldmund has become appreciative of an element of spirituality in love. In loving all women, young or old, he dedicates himself to love as a principle.

His concept of love having grown more mature, love again becomes Goldmund's foremost experiential value. Goldmund gradually tears himself loose from the world of art.

## Death and Desire.

The growth of the concept of love leads for Goldmund to an expansion of the image of the Great Mother. "He knew...that his road led to the Mother, to lust and death" (italics supplied).

## Goldmund's Love for Narcissus.

In the death aspect of the Mother image lies the foremost explanation of Goldmund's love for Narcissus. Narcissus is not afflicted by the sting of death; to Goldmund he is serenely beyond the sufferance of the transient. Goldmund, however, must seek the Great Mother, even though she spells death. But when Goldmund is dying, he has fully accepted me Great Mother as a harbinger of destruction. Narcissus' imperviousness to death has become a liability. "But how will you die when the time comes, Narcissus, since you do not have a mother?" Narcissus of course has a mother in the literal sense, but there is no efficacy of the Mother image in his soul. Thus as the representative of spirit and permanence, Narcissus does not know how to die. In dying Goldmund's love for Narcissus turns therefore to pity.

### Art and the Father and Mother Worlds.

Artistic creativity can bring only brief happiness. The warring factions in Goldmund's soul, love for a free life and the attraction of a disciplined permanent form of existence, cannot be brought to permanent peace. Only in a supra-personal sense can there be union. Art, abstractly considered, is a meeting of two opposing worlds. "Art was a union of the Father and Mother Worlds of spirit and blood. Art could begin in the most sensual sphere and lead to the most abstract or begin the pure world of ideas and end in the bleeding flesh."

### But to Goldmund this union is only a possibility for the "artist."

In his own life the call of freedom, his "most essential need," must prevail. At the completion of the St. John's statue, Master Niklaus' world, the bishop's city, is a prison for Goldmund. There is no image in his mind that he is ready to make into a statue. "That longed-for image of images, the figure of the Mother of Men, was out of reach for him."

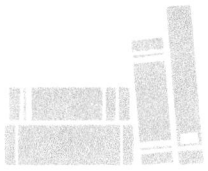

# NARCISSUS AND GOLDMUND

## TEXTUAL ANALYSIS

### CHAPTER TWELVE

.....................................................................

The Call of the Mother. As was the case when Goldmund left Mariabronn, the actual decision to leave is arrived at slowly. Watching fish die in their barrels at the market helps him to define his feelings and make a decision. He identifies with the beautiful fish, whose capture and death struggle leave the crude burghers absolutely untouched. They want the fish on their plates, Goldmund wishes to see them alive, in their natural element, the water. Water **imagery**, as has already been mentioned, is plentiful in this novel. It is a symbol of the transient life Goldmund is meant to live. Water and the fish in it stand for the very opposite of the fixed, urban, settled and imprisoned existence that would be Goldmund's lot if he stayed in the city. His empathy with the fish incenses him against the burghers. The peace of mind he thought he had had in their contented town was an illusion.

This falling away of the illusion turns into a sense of death and suffering within Goldmund. He "stares into the abyss."

The aspect of suffering and death has been on the ascendency in Goldmund's life since the murder of Viktor about whom Goldmund now muses a great deal. The moments during which he can recapture the simple joy of living have become rare. The joy of achievement, his acceptance by Master Niklaus as an equal, is only a "wilted flower" for him.

The abyss into which Goldmund stares is not empty. In the middle of his thoughts of despair he has a powerful vision of the Great Mother. She has a smile both "beautiful" and "gruesome." She looks at birth and death, and to her everything has the same meaning. The dying fish in the market are as close to her as is Goldmund; Viktor's bones are as dear to her as is Master Niklaus' daughter. After this vision, Goldmund's feelings are clear. The burghers and their world can "go to hell." He goes to Master Niklaus to tell him how he feels, but Master Niklaus considers Goldmund's depression only temporary. It is to him the emptiness an artist feels when the creative process is over. He asks Goldmund to come back in a few days.

Two Types of Beauty. Again Goldmund muses about fish and water. Their beauty seems to be formless, like images of the soul. The essential feature of this beauty is mystery. The beauty of a work of art, on the other hand, is precise, clear and ascertainable in its form. A great work of art has definite form and also the aura of mystery.

For Goldmund the most formidable image of the soul is the Universal Mother. It is natural, then, that he has the desire to capture this image in stone or wood. The image of the Mother is to him the supreme image of life. It alone contains the entire spectrum in terms of the opposites of birth and death, joy and pain, life and destruction.

In order to create her external image, Goldmund must follow her road. He must experience life further. He feels that this is the goal and meaning of his life. When Master Niklaus offers him a master's diploma in the guild, the hand of his daughter in marriage and his shop after his death, Goldmund is therefore not tempted to remain. He leaves the city.

### The Growth of Caritas (Compassion).

As Goldmund is about to leave the city early in the morning, the crippled daughter of the family where he lodges is up to bid him good-by. She is very sad to see him go. Goldmund is appreciative and kisses her. It is obvious Goldmund does not kiss her out of desire. This is the first incident in which Goldmund's contact with girls reveals a note of compassion. Since Goldmund's life now stands under the aegis of death, there is an emphasis on pain and suffering. As the awareness of death leads him to the awareness of suffering, it also, by means of identification with those who suffer, leads to compassion.

# NARCISSUS AND GOLDMUND

## TEXTUAL ANALYSIS

### CHAPTER THIRTEEN

The Glories of the Life of the Wayfarer. As Goldmund learns again to live the homeless life of the traveler, Hesse gives that life characteristics that make it appear superior to the existence of the settled. Goldmund is the brother to the animals and thus partakes of their innocence. He lives from moment to moment and accepts whatever God's world has to offer. But although he is a child at heart, his life is not idyllic. He is lonely and has a deadly enemy in the house-owner, who hates and fears him, for the wanderer reminds him that all life is transitory, that everything will die.

Patterns Repeated. Important events in the earlier phase of Goldmund's life on the road are repeated in this chapter. The first settlement described in detail to which Goldmund comes in both phases is a farmer's hut. The families are almost identical; both consist of an old woman, a farmer, his wife and a small boy. The second family, however, has an additional child.

Goldmund also finds another traveling companion, Robert, whose background, like Goldmund's and Viktor's, ties him to the world of religion. He has made a pilgrimage to Rome.

Patterns Modified. The family Goldmund knew earlier had been alive and healthy. The family in this chapter is dead of the plague. In his relationship with Viktor, Goldmund had been the submissive partner; in his relationship with Robert, Goldmund is dominant.

The Significance of the Changes in the Patterns. As Goldmund's life falls more and more under the aegis of the Mother, there is an increase in the threat of death indicated by the condition of the second family. Goldmund reacts to this threat by asserting himself in terms of dominance in social contacts.

In the phase of his life up to the murder of Viktor Goldmund by and large assumed a role of submission. Obvious elements of dominance were the cloister and Narcissus. But there were others as well. Goldmund's girls ran back to their husbands; the husbands' dominance exceeded Goldmund's powers as a lover. The knight of the castle was a father figure against whom Goldmund was shown as submissive. Being ejected from the castle, Goldmund meekly followed the commands of the "master." Goldmund is under the threat of the sword the knight carries, yet he does not assert himself enough to run away from the old knight as he easily could have done. In the Viktor episode Goldmund asserts himself for the first time. With few exceptions he maintains the upper hand both literally and figuratively during the rest of his life.

Even in a rigorous environment like Master Niklaus' household, Goldmund is not submissive, but does as he pleases.

When he had entered the dwelling of the farmer after the Lise **episode**, he had to submit to scrutiny by the farmer and to his decision that he sleep outside. When Goldmund enters the pestilential hut in this chapter, he is the one who scrutinizes the farmer's family and is in command. He orders the frightened Robert about. He calls him "little boy" and takes on the role of head of the family when he, Lene and Robert live together.

The Plague. As Goldmund moves about in the pestilential country, he has visions of the Universal Mother. Her face is "pale" and "gigantic." Her eyes are like Medusa's, her smile heavy with suffering and death. The Black Death is the supreme manifestation of the power of the Great Mother. Though it frightens Goldmund, it also fascinates him deeply because he recognizes the Universal Mother in it. Thus the plague has an aura of grandeur and even "nobility" to him.

# NARCISSUS AND GOLDMUND

## TEXTUAL ANALYSIS

### CHAPTER FOURTEEN

Reign of Chaos. Goldmund reaches in this chapter the deepest level of despair in his life. In the confession he bitterly accuses God of having made the world badly. Significantly, Goldmund finds that there is no priest behind the curtain to hear him and so he receives no answer or comfort. Lene dies of the plague. Goldmund kills the marauder who attempted to rape her and who infected her. Robert, his companion, vanishes. Even the girl Rebekka, who as a Jewess is blamed for the plague and who is rescued by Goldmund from being killed like her father, bitterly rejects Goldmund. She sees only the lust in Goldmund, not his wish to care for her. Rebekka would rather die, than be Goldmund's lover. Horrors of the plague are everywhere.

Control of Chaos. In the depth of despair, Goldmund remembers an antidote: the world of art: He longs to return to Master Niklaus to craft some images, wishing to objectify his experiences of horror in art. He feels works of art are "an infinite comfort, a triumphant victory over death and despair."

**Theme** of Caritas (Compassion). In the face of death and suffering, Goldmund's attachment to others is further suffused by feelings of compassion. He nurses the dying Lene to the end. To Rebekka he says, "I only want to see you and care for you." He also assumes the burden of caring for a young child rather than abandoning him. His sense of caring, no doubt, is to a large degree born out of the horrors around him. But significantly, it is stated that Goldmund's attitude toward death and the plague is not entirely one of fear. Rather, his relationship to death is mainly one of intimacy.

Art and the Mother World. In the dynamics of life and death, in the spectacle of transitoriness, art is a fixed point of reference. It is an element of permanence, created by the human spirit. But Goldmund's highest aspiration as an artist is the crafting of the image of the Great Mother. Thus his fixed point of reference is a concept that in itself stands for transitoriness. Goldmund, then, has as his highest goal as an artist the glorification of the law of all existence: impermanence. Goldmund's destiny is to live and die, to be in accord with the dual image of the Great Mother, the giver of life and death.

# NARCISSUS AND GOLDMUND

## TEXTUAL ANALYSIS

### CHAPTER FIFTEEN

Homecoming. Goldmund retraces the route of his journey, returning to the bishop's city and ultimately to Mariabronn. After his experiences with the plague, the city seems a haven of security to him. Though it had been ravished by the plague, life there has returned to normal. Goldmund once again is attracted to the notion of domesticity, especially to the opportunity for artistic creation that the city offers. Though the plague has decimated the population, in certain aspects the city has not changed. Its citizens are as unfeeling as ever. In Master Niklaus' house, too, the essential features have not changed. It is still a cold house to Goldmund, the outsider. But the coldness now is that of death. Master Niklaus, sterile in life in his single-mindedness as a provider, dies in his attempts to save his daughter for whom alone he had worked. Lisbeth survived the plague, but her beauty is gone. Though the burghers tread along as insensitively as ever, to Goldmund the city is a place of gloom. He recognizes the imprint of death everywhere.

Before engaging in the pursuit of Agnes, Goldmund spends a few days in hectic drawing. Death is his main motif. In this brief intermezzo with art, Goldmund comes to terms with the horrors of the plague behind him, as during his first stay in the city he had come to terms with his relationship to Narcissus. In art, Goldmund objectifies death. He gains some control over and distance from his experience of death by subjecting it to artistic form. This done, Goldmund's mind can be somewhat free; he can abandon himself to the joys of love once again. But death soon returns to his consciousness. He knows full well he is risking his life when he courts the magnificent Agnes.

### The Apotheosis of the Lover.

Agnes is the absolute high point in Goldmund's love life. She is unlike any other woman Goldmund has ever loved. She is the most stunning and voluptuous female he has ever seen, also the most inaccessible and dangerous to love. Loving her is the culmination of all his love experiences. In her, Goldmund comes face to face with the meaning of his life. Agnes, he realizes, matches his features; she is his mirror image. In her dangerousness and fierceness on one hand, her radiant beauty and voluptuousness on the other, Agnes is the final and supreme variant of the Great Mother image in Goldmund's love life.

Every woman Goldmund had loved has to be seen within the context of the Great Mother image. They all had been phases in Goldmund's quest for her. In Agnes, he comes closest to his goal. She is also the one woman who reminds him of the image of his own mother. Although the consciousness of death suffuses it, this encounter with Agnes, in contrast with the later one shortly before Goldmund's death, places the accent on her as a life giver. Agnes is the only woman who wants a child by Goldmund. His powerful craving for life in the face of his execution for having been caught in Agnes' chambers is strengthened, no doubt, by his love experiences with her.

# NARCISSUS AND GOLDMUND

## TEXTUAL ANALYSIS

### CHAPTER SIXTEEN

..................................................

Stocktaking and Thematic Recapitulation. In terms of the life of the senses, the Agnes experience represents Goldmund's final learning phase. But through it he has reached not only the high point of "carnal knowledge" but also a higher level of reflective consciousness. The stocktaking of his life assumes the form of thematic recapitulation.

As Goldmund awaits the second night of love-making with Agnes, he goes out into the hills overlooking the city. He rests near some burial mounds and perceives his past life in the perspective of Transitoriness. Everything he ever held dear is lost or dead. He longs for the Permanence that artistic creation leads to. The images flowing through his soul are not enough, though they provide him with Pain and Joy. The schoolboy Goldmund never was content with the Learning at Mariabronn. Now as a mature man, he has gained full Awareness of the meaning of the life of the senses, the life for which he was destined. It is precariously open to death. The only alternative open to him would have been a life of disciplined Artistic Creation. But such an existence would have implied the death of the senses. Goldmund realizes there would have been no satisfactory middle ground for him. He recognizes that all life is based on Dichotomies. Life's dynamics implies that aligning oneself with one side results in a Longing for the other. But although longing is the consequence of the eternal split in the universe, it is to Goldmund nonetheless a positive value. All that is "beautiful and sacred" comes from it. Longing, then, is the only possible form of Union for opposites. Although Goldmund accepts the dualities of life intellectually, he is deeply perturbed. Emotionally, Goldmund has to develop further. The spectrum of experiences, though in love it has reached its summation in Agnes, must still be widened. The ultimate experience, the meeting with and understanding of the Great Mother, is still before him. It will appease his Longing and let him die on a note of Union.

But having been caught in Agnes' chambers, Goldmund does not yet resign himself to dying. He has a vision of his mother in the dungeon and is able to fall asleep peacefully. But as he wakes up, his desire to stay alive returns violently.

Since the life of the lover and wayfarer has taken Goldmund to the door of death, since it spells impermanence in itself, Goldmund's longing for life must find a focus that signals permanence. Narcissus and his world will provide this form.

When Goldmund had lived the wayfarer's life in extremis he had ended the phase as the murderer of Viktor; he has also lived the lover's life in extremis and now almost becomes the murderer of Narcissus. Goldmund refrains from murder only when he recognizes that the priest, who enters his cell, is Narcissus. His willingness to kill a priest who is about to provide absolution from his sins carries even graver implications than had the murder of Viktor. There he killed a man who was about to kill him. Here he is willing to kill a man who is about to save him. For to a priest the saving of the soul is more important than the saving of the body. It is his love for Narcissus that prevents Goldmund from becoming a murderer again. The power of friendship saves both the lives of Narcissus and Goldmund.

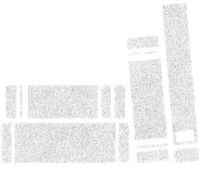

# NARCISSUS AND GOLDMUND

## TEXTUAL ANALYSIS

### CHAPTER SEVENTEEN

Renewal of Friendship. When Goldmund recognizes Narcissus in the dungeon he is shaken to the root of his being. But nonetheless he immediately reacts in the manner he knows Narcissus expects. He behaves as Narcissus would; he makes a supreme effort to control his emotions. He falls back into the ironic and stubborn tones in which he used to speak to Narcissus as a youth. The relationship of student and teacher is immediately reestablished. Narcissus is in a position of superiority. Goldmund even fails to shock Narcissus with the revelation that he has killed before. But Goldmund evens the score a bit by demonstrating his kind of superiority when he reveals that he has become a sculptor and that he anticipated Narcissus' new name, St. John, when he gave it to the Narcissus statue. The notion of death unites them further. Narcissus, too, had experienced death when the plague invaded the cloister. Not only do the two friends share the experience of death, but their love for one another overrules their deepest commitments. Goldmund's love for Narcissus had triumphed over his craving to stay alive at all costs when he faced execution; Narcissus' love for Goldmund had caused him to sacrifice his duty to the cloister. He had to make important concessions to the governor at the expense of his order to receive a pardon for Goldmund.

Dichotomy. Though the motif of union is clearly present in the dynamics of Goldmund's and Narcissus' renewed friendship, the more basic motif of contrast is in the foreground. Goldmund attacks Narcissus for being ultimately in agreement with the order of the world which to Goldmund is fundamentally evil. Goldmund is picking an argument on Narcissus' home front, the arena of theology, and is quickly put down. Narcissus explains to him that one may feel the world as a creation is imperfect, but against it one must infer a perfect creator. Only the concept of a perfect creator can explain that man can envision justice and perfection. Narcissus proves that Goldmund still thinks in images and not in thoughts; Goldmund is therefore in a sense disqualified as a debator. The world of feeling and images is transitory; thus Goldmund cannot arrive at the idea of permanence that only thought can give.

Goldmund, however, can counter with the revelation that he has created art, something permanent, in contrast to the temporality of life. The true artist perceives the basic image, the essence of the object he creates, in his soul. Thus he does not merely copy surface reality but captures its spiritual component. Therefore the essence of art is spirit. At this juncture in the dynamics of friendship, the argument returns to the note of union.

Narcissus is joyous over Goldmund's line of thought and accepts its validity. Now the two friends are on the same ground. The artist, Narcissus concedes, has the same faculty as the thinker in that both share access to the world of ideas. The "basic image" is the same as what the philosopher calls an idea. It is spirit, it is mind. Goldmund's acknowledgment of spirit and mind as basic to creative art is to Narcissus a "confession." Through art Goldmund has aligned himself with the world of mind and thus can be a legitimate member of the cloister community. Narcissus invites him to set up a workshop in the cloister.

To be sure, their friendship is first and foremost based on love. This love is personal and transcends ideological allegiances. In view of the dungeon incident it implies for both a compromising of their values. Narcissus had to ignore his duty to the order, Goldmund his desire for freedom. Now their friendship is based also on a shared spiritual commitment. For both the mind is the essence of the world and their ground of being. Unfortunately, the equation holds true only if Goldmund, the person, were identical at all times to Goldmund, the artist. Goldmund's commitment to art is, however, not permanent.

# NARCISSUS AND GOLDMUND

## TEXTUAL ANALYSIS

### CHAPTER EIGHTEEN

..................................................

Homecoming. Although Goldmund experiences his homecoming at first in terms of sounds and images, i.e., through the senses, it becomes more meaningful through art. He sees the cloister as an artist, perceiving the beauty of the statues, paintings and architecture. Through the perspective of art, of ordered unity, he understands the larger unity of the cloister as an institution. Everything in it serves this unity. Goldmund feels that he himself must become a part of it. He wishes to overcome his position as outsider. He wants to make a general confession and be received as a lay brother. In his eyes Narcissus has grown "strangely tall" as me center of the majestic unity that is Mariabronn. He becomes Goldmund's teacher again, providing him with the reasons why he now can be accepted in the cloister whereas as a youth he had to be encouraged to leave. Those who are persons of feeling, yet live the life of thought, must become mystics, Narcissus believes. Such would have been Goldmund's fate had he not left the cloister as a youth. Mystics are dangerous; they are in Narcissus' eyes people without tools with which to realize themselves. They are doomed to be unhappy. They should have become poets or artists. For that reason, Narcissus reminds Goldmund, he had encouraged him to leave school. He knew that only then would Goldmund be able to fulfill himself.

Goldmund now can understand what self-realization means. It implies that man must submit to the process of "becoming," by which he moves closer to perfect "being." Narcissus, too, had to 'realize' himself but judges his road to have been easier than Goldmund's. A cloister, he says, holds fewer hazards than the open road. But though thinking is less dangerous than wandering, the thinker who needs little experience and might be said to be engaged in pure thought is nonetheless very useful. He must not be seen as someone who solves empty problems. On the contrary, he constantly wishes to apply his thinking to reality, to the problems of other human beings. As Goldmund had to apply his feeling to the creation of works of art, Narcissus applies his thought to the problems of the cloister. Both processes yield results. Contrary to the young Goldmund, the artist Goldmund is able to grasp why thinking without images, why logic is useful. He can understand it by the process of analogy predicated on his own life in which experience led to application in art. After Goldmund passes the 'initiation rites' to Mariabronn, he has the feeling that "only now his true life was about to begin."

Sculpturing for Mariabronn. Note that the ambitious sculpture Goldmund envisions has a dual aspect; one part is to represent the world, the other the word of god. In terms of the novel's structure, the sculpture restates the fundamental dualities and harmonies already encountered. The word, the logos, the mind, redeems the world of temporality and sensuality, as conversely, the world yearns for salvation through the spirit.

Self-realization. As work on the sculpture progresses, Goldmund gains more self-confidence. He now feels "big" enough to ask for confession. Narcissus chastises him not for his wild ways of the past but for not having said his prayers enough and for not having been to confession enough. In terms of character analysis, Narcissus still understands Goldmund better than Goldmund does himself. The sins of commission all were essential to Goldmund's self-realization; he, in effect, has only sins of omission. The penance Narcissus describes for Goldmund is designed to aid him in developing a disciplined work life.

Life as an Insider. While Goldmund is at work on the sculpture, for a brief period the life of order makes him happy. Religious ritual now satisfies him as carousing had while he worked under Master Niklaus. The second 'art phase' in his life, then, indicates a higher level in Goldmund's existence.

Art and Friendship. Among the many figures of his project is an evangelist modeled after Abbot Daniel: Narcissus' reaction to it intimates the joy and love of friendship. Narcissus feels that now he fully knows who Goldmund is. To Narcissus, he has reached a high point of self-realization. As Goldmund sees that his friend understands the sculpture, he is proud and deeply moved. Art, though it cannot unite the friends in an ultimate sense, has nonetheless an efficacious bonding function. This is emphasized by the specific implication of the art work before them. It represents the Abbot Daniel, a man of harmony who had character traits of both Goldmund and Narcissus.

# NARCISSUS AND GOLDMUND

## TEXTUAL ANALYSIS

### CHAPTER NINETEEN

The Call of Life; Recurrence and Transience. Significantly, while under the spell of the initiation into the religious life, Goldmund works first on the second part of his ambitious sculpturing project. It is the part of the logos, of mind. When he takes up the first part that is to represent the world, Goldmund's life style changes. He again is attracted by the world of the senses and he begins to foray away from the cloister. But while he is at work on the sculpture, he becomes Narcissus' teacher. It is the student, however, who verbalizes what is being taught. Narcissus admits that he used to look down at art and that he valued it less highly than thinking and science. Now he realizes that there are many roads to knowledge and that the path of the mind is perhaps not even the best one. Since art is the fruit of the life of the senses, Narcissus has legitimized Goldmund's past life. This gives Goldmund added impetus to revert to his old life style. He is afraid that his life will be like Master Niklaus' if its present course in the cloister continues. He has grown tame and domesticated. Worst of all, he finds himself roaming around the countryside looking not for live adventure, but for the memories of his past experiences.

After hearing a rumor that Agnes is in the vicinity, he decides to break away from Mariabronn completely, to wander and love women once more. During this brief period of decision, Goldmund carves a statue of Lydia. His love for her is analogous to his love for Mariabronn and Narcissus. Though it is deep and sincere, it is fated not to be consummated; it remains incomplete.

Innocence. Narcissus must let Goldmund go, even though his leaving means the recurrence of Goldmund's wild and lustful life. Goldmund is to him like an innocent child, much more innocent than Narcissus feels he is himself. Goldmund's innocence rests on his honest giving in to his instincts and emotions, a process largely without reflection. There is in it little of the notion of sin and guilt. In this perspective of innocence, Goldmund is mutatis mutandis in the same position as he was when he first left the cloister as a youth. He must go in search of sensual experience.

# NARCISSUS AND GOLDMUND

## TEXTUAL ANALYSIS

### CHAPTER TWENTY

...........................................................

The Call of Death. When Goldmund returns for the last time to the cloister, he is labeled a "false" Goldmund. Indeed, the man who comes back is no longer the lover, the strong, virile creature. He is old, spent, exhausted and sick. Goldmund has fallen deeply under the spell of death. He looks at himself in the mirror but is not horrified. He can accept his approaching death because he feels the greatest joy is still awaiting him. He believes he is still "on the road to his mother." The meeting with her is a death that will take him to "non-being" and to "innocence." It will bring him the happiness of "fulfilled love."

Dichotomy and Union. Only death can provide a consummate union with an opposite for Goldmund. His fulfillment will be the meeting with his mother, the end of the road toward self-realization. In life, however, there can be only an approximation of fulfillment. With regard to the friendship between Narcissus and Goldmund, Hesse expresses this idea through the device of timing. Early in the novel, when Goldmund had stroked

Narcissus' hair, Narcissus was embarrassed by it. Now, in the final chapter, Narcissus kisses his dying friend's hair and confesses his love for him. This time Goldmund, even though a man of the widest experience, is slightly embarrassed. As the two friends talk of their love for one another, the only witness is the Lydia-madonna, the statue symbolizing non-consummation.

The Meeting of the Mother. After Goldmund is rejected by Agnes, the foremost variant of the Great Mother image as a life-and-love giver in Goldmund's mature life, he returns to his own mother in a vision. She, his literal life giver, cuddles him in her lap after his fall off the horse and initiates him into dying. Goldmund lies in a brook after his fall; the baptismal element of water is present once more. Goldmund's mother merges with the face of the Great Mother in the clouds. Thus it is ultimately the Great Mother who tempts Goldmund into dying. She is Goldmund's mother when she reaches between his ribs to take his heart out. In this image Hesse seems to be using elements of the Garden of Eden myth. Through Eve, created of Adam's rib, temptation, sin, carnal knowledge and death came into the world. "Mother Eve" tempts Goldmund for the last time. She lures him to death. Goldmund readily submits to her spell. Hesse's twist of the myth is, however, that to Goldmund death is not punishment, but deliverance and happiness.

The Great Mother, Art, and Death. Goldmund had cherished the wish of someday creating a statue of the Great Mother. Now, however, it is the Great Mother who shapes him. The Great Mother, transitoriness, and therewith Goldmund's way of life, have the final authority in the novel. Art, that which makes the transient permanent, does not. Implied in this is the inferiority of Narcissus' form of existence, which is dedicated to permanence.

As Goldmund dies, his final words show concern for Narcissus: "But how will you die some day, Narcissus, since you do not have a mother? Without a mother, you cannot love, without a mother, you cannot die." Goldmund consummates the union with the Mother. His friendship with Narcissus, in contrast, must remain incomplete. Goldmund's final statement once again points to the unbridgeable dichotomy between the two friends as it also establishes Goldmund's superiority over Narcissus. Whereas Narcissus' love for Goldmund may not be love at all, for without a mother one cannot love, Goldmund has found the Mother; he can love and he can die fulfilled.

# NARCISSUS AND GOLDMUND

## CHARACTER ANALYSIS

### FEMALE CHARACTERS

All of the women associated with Goldmund serve the purpose of defining him or propelling him forward on the road to the Mother. In each of them he finds a part of the "eternal feminine." His last lover, the beautiful Agnes, the governor's mistress, is a mirror image of himself and reminds him of his own mother. She is the culmination of all his love affairs. Significantly, she is the woman with the greatest social standing of the women in the book - though, being only a governor's mistress, there is a suggestion of illicitness reminiscent of Goldmund's own mother. Lise, Goldmund's first lover, is a gypsy, and thus on a very low level of medieval society. Goldmund, as the medieval cloister scholar, comes to her with considerable social standing. To Agnes, he comes as a "beggar," a non-person in the societal sense. His social standing, if anything, decreases during his life. In the perspective of the life of the senses, however, there is growth in Goldmund. But this development is not linear. There are a few women who disrupt it in not contributing to Goldmund's sensual fulfillment. These unfulfilled relationships have a dialectic bearing on Goldmund's consummated liaisons. They put his growth into focus as sensuality since they provide the alternative of a more spiritual love which Goldmund rejects.

## Goldmund's Mother

Though she does not appear personally in the novel, Goldmund's memories of her provide a fundamental impetus in his life. Goldmund's mother had been a wild and beautiful creature who after a few years of marriage had rejected her domestication and reverted to a life of seduction and reputed witchery. Since she had brought shame to the family, Goldmund's father had suppressed Goldmund's memories of her. Significantly, she is of noble, yet poor birth. It helps us to see that in her as well as Goldmund's sensual dissipations there is nonetheless an "aristocratic" element.

The rediscovery of Goldmund's memories of his mother, prompted by Narcissus, is such a crucial experience for Goldmund that he faints as the recollections well up from the subconscious past the censor. They are essentially the physical image of his mother, which recurring again and again, ultimately merges with the image of the Great Mother. The last time the image appears to Goldmund, it is again in connection with a state of unconsciousness, as Goldmund had fallen into the brook. Thus the Mother has the function of aligning the subconscious with the conscious in Goldmund. It is the Mother World that gives Goldmund the depth that Narcissus cannot attain and which he envies. Without it, Goldmund tells him, he cannot die. A true acceptance of death must come from the Mother's sphere, the soul; to the mind, by which Narcissus lives, death is unfathomable and unacceptable.

## Lise

The gypsy girl Lise is Goldmund's first lover. She is a creature of the woods and fields who seems totally undomesticated. Yet, paradoxically, she returns to her husband instead of becoming Goldmund's companion. With the exception of Lene none of the women Goldmund meets wishes to follow him into the world. Though some of them might be free and untamed creatures, they are nonetheless fundamentally different from Goldmund. He must roam because he is in search of the Mother. The women need not roam, for they are, figuratively speaking, the Mother.

## Lydia

A knight's daughter, Lydia is a very proud girl who desires Goldmund but will not sleep with him. On occasion, she lies next to him in bed, but she does not let him touch her. Lydia, however, introduces Goldmund to a new aspect of love. Besides desire, there is a spiritual bond between them. It is Lydia who chooses to develop this bond. It gives her insights into Goldmund's nature that no other girl in the book can equal. She recognizes that he is destined to be a wanderer and that he has no home. His eyes, though they appear happy, reveal to her a deeper unhappiness which results from his awareness that everything is transient. Lydia, in contrast, values her home. Knowing that she belongs to the feudal aristocracy gives her strength. She will make love only to the man she marries. Since she cannot marry Goldmund their relationship is hopeless. When it is on the point of getting out of hand, she confesses it to her father. In Lydia, Hesse confronts Goldmund with a girl who is, in fact, a part of the world of the Father and thus, the world of Narcissus. There is no mother in the family. The knight is somewhat of a scholar. He commands the castle and is a paternal figure to Goldmund. The entire castle world is one of order. Thus, Lydia, in her commitment to her father and her class, is ultimately committed to an idea. The patriarchal chivalric class is as much a construct of mind and order as is Narcissus' cloister.

## Lisbeth

In a slightly altered sense, what applied to Lydia also is true of Lisbeth, the beautiful daughter of Master Niklaus. She, too, has aristocratic reserve and is even more haughty and less approachable than Lydia. She is a member of the burgher class, the new "aristocracy" of the age. She would marry Goldmund, if her father decreed it. But to be eligible Goldmund would have to become a citizen in good standing. In contrast to the chivalric class, to which one had to be born, the burgher elite permitted outsiders to enter through marriage if they had accumulated the proper merit. Master Niklaus is the strong ruler of the household. Lisbeth is shown to us in the process of carrying out his orders. Again, there is no mother in the family.

## Rebekka

Through her religion, the Jewish girl Rebekka, whom Goldmund helps to escape from her persecutors, also is aligned with a patriarchal order. Though Goldmund offers to protect her, though she is all alone in the world and in great danger, she rejects Goldmund as a lover and thus loses him as her protector. Her allegiance is to her father who had been killed by the Christians. His "last fingernail" is worth more to her than all the Christians put together. Again, there is no mention of a mother.

## Summary Comment on Lydia, Lisbeth, and Rebekka

All three girls have a primary allegiance to the Father World. They are not immune to Goldmund's charms, but their ultimate responsibility is to their fathers. The love they can offer goes beyond the sensual, it carries with it the notion of class or religion, thus an element of spirit. The spiritual component is especially pronounced in his love for Lydia and Rebekka. They are the only women Goldmund feels he has truly loved. But when he has to make a choice between love and desire, he nonetheless opts for desire. Though these girls fascinate him deeply, they further his quest for self-realization only in making him aware of the primacy of the sensual in his nature. For example, when he is lying in bed next to Lydia, the two are joined by her younger sister, the curious and jealous Julie. Goldmund diverts his attention to Julie since she permits him to touch her. He, then, is willing to betray Lydia, the girl he professes to love, in her very presence.

The Father World to which these girls belong is ultimately defined in the novel through the figure of Narcissus. Although Narcissus is absent during the center section of the novel, Goldmund remains figuratively in touch with him.

## Lene

Goldmund enters into a sort of common law marriage with Lene who succeeds in holding him longer than any other female in the book. The childlike Robert completes the family. But it is the threat of the plague, the social chaos prevalent all around that provide the impetus for the establishment of a family. Hesse seems to make a comment on the nature of marriage as a reaction to circumstantial exigencies. Marriage, in other words, is a way of shielding oneself from the threats of life. Although Goldmund has witnessed every horror the plague has generated, he has no intention of staying with Lene. He will let his basic wandering instincts reign.

## Marie

Although described as having very beautiful eyes, Marie is the one girl who does not stir any feelings of desire in Goldmund. She has a limp; the suggestion is that Goldmund does not feel attracted to her because she is slightly crippled. To Goldmund, who after all is sensitive to beauty, Marie's beautiful eyes should offset her deformity. He should respond to her wooing. Marie, then, constitutes an indictment against Goldmund. Female beauty rules out anatomical flaws. In seeing it in anatomical terms, he sees it in an erotic rather than spiritual perspective. But Goldmund gives Marie friendliness in turn for her love for him. There is a note of caritas, of compassion in his feeling for her.

## Agnes

More so than in any others of his lovers, the life giving and the dangerous components in the female are obvious in Agnes. She dominates Goldmund. She leaves the city on horseback; he follows her on foot. She indicates to him the great risk of loving her. In fact, in the affair with Agnes the closeness of love and aggression becomes visible. She smiles a "challenge" at Goldmund, after which their love-making is described as "combat." Agnes needs to be conquered. Goldmund has to penetrate the castle in which she lives to meet her. She is more than a match for Goldmund. Indeed, she is his undoing. Her primary allegiance is, like Goldmund's, the life of the senses. She thus defeats Goldmund on his home ground when she rejects him in the end.

## THE MALE CHARACTERS

Among the father figures in the novel, Goldmund's own father is the most negative variant. He ordains Goldmund for a cloister life and through it intends to have Goldmund atone for the sins of his mother. Thus he sacrifices Goldmund to his concept of Christianity.

### The Knight

Lydia's father is a more positive character than Goldmund's father. He is fond of learning and impressed with Goldmund's knowledge of Greek. He had forayed into the world as a young man, but had returned to lead the orderly life of a country squire. In his fondness for books and learning we can associate him with Narcissus. He is a father figure who has been in sympathy with Goldmund's world and now wishes to chronicle it.

### Master Niklaus

As a solid burgher, Master Niklaus at best tolerates Goldmund's shiftless and carousing nature. He intends to buy it off by offering Goldmund a master's diploma and his daughter. Since Goldmund is extremely talented, Master Niklaus believes his commitment to art will predispose him to the acceptance of the bribe. Of course, Master Niklaus is wrong. Since he is such a staid establishment type himself, he misjudges Goldmund. There is a similarity to Goldmund's father in that Master Niklaus too is willing to sacrifice his child to a system. In one case it would be sacrifice to Christian dogma, in the other to professionalism. It deserves to be pointed out in this context that Narcissus, also a father figure of course, is not willing to sacrifice Goldmund to the monastic order, as we might expect from a man who fervently wishes to serve it. He does not force Goldmund into a mold of the "father's" choosing, but directs him to find his own.

## Abbot Daniel

The Abbot provides a significant counterweight to both Narcissus and Goldmund as literary figures. They are both highly extraordinary, indeed extreme personality types. Abbot Daniel, on the other hand, is neither outstandingly intelligent nor extremely sensitive; his gifts are not spectacular. In fact, his analytical intelligence is capable of failing him completely, for example when he calls the coldly logical Narcissus a visionary and romantic. But as the Abbot lacks both the high degree of Goldmund's sensitivity and Narcissus' profound cerebrality, he nonetheless has the gift of wisdom. Judgment and compassion, feeling and thinking merge harmoniously in him. Since he is a very kind man he worries about those of whom he is in charge. Still, there is also a serenity about him that borders on the saintly.

From the perspective of literary structure, the personality of Abbot Daniel provides a fixed point of reference against the highly dynamic relationship of Goldmund and Narcissus who are "two halves in search of one another." When we compare the Abbot with Narcissus, he seems to be a Goldmund type. (As a Goldmund type he is also an introductory foil to Goldmund in the first chapter.) He feels rather than knows. He tells the all too perfect Narcissus to misbehave a little. The Abbot is not a good scholar. Though the learned monks love him, some of them evidence the same intellectual condescension toward the Abbot that Narcissus displays toward Goldmund. Conversely, when we compare Abbot Daniel with Goldmund, his similarity to Narcissus becomes apparent. He has a high developed sense of service and is a man of order and discipline. The balance and harmoniousness of Abbot Daniel's personality seems at first to expose both Narcissus and Goldmund as insufficiently developed, "unreal" characters, as bloodless types. But in view of the very fact that the Abbot Daniel can relate to them very deeply, and they to him, this judgment must be reconsidered. Since the Abbot is so "real," since he is such a warm and kind personality, the objects of his love and kindness come alive, too.

## Narcissus

If literature has produced a quintessential lover of the world of ideas, it is Narcissus. Ideas are true and sacred to him, systems and dogma are not. He tells Goldmund that it would not matter to him if Goldmund burned down the cloister in the course of self-fulfillment. Since he loves ideas, Narcissus can steer Goldmund toward self-realization, knowing full well that by doing so he will drive his beloved friend from his side. This is the meaning of Narcissus' spiritual love for Goldmund. It far outweighs his physical attraction for him. The homosexual overtones in their relationship are not to be read as "censured passion" or "controlled lust" in Narcissus.

When Narcissus is called the other half of Goldmund in the novel, Hesse does not indicate lifelessness of character in both figures. The suggestion is rather that if both halves were put together, they would form an ideal personality. German writers are predisposed to the presentation of personality and identity quests in terms of polar opposites mainly in emulation of Goethe's brilliant model, *Faust.* Looking at Faust, perhaps the most prototypical symbol of modern man in literature, we find that his personality problems are seen as "two souls" at war with one another within one personality. Here in *Narcissus and Goldmund,* the two souls are two figures. They are even called "two halves" in the novel. But they are linked by love and yearning. This is the perspective in which we must understand the problem. Love and yearning for the other half is a craving for inner harmony, for peace of the soul in both Goldmund and Narcissus. The friends' love and yearning for one another is their psyches' therapy for inner conflict. By making us think of Goldmund and Narcissus as halves in search for one another, Hesse in fact leads us to realize what makes them truly "real" people: their quest for peace of soul and mind.

But Goldmund and Narcissus are "real" people not only by interpretive inference; they are in fact full-fledged, self-assertive human egos. Whenever the two friends argue, there exists a subtle yet powerful tension between them. There is between them a multi-shaded dialectic of assertion and concession that could not exist if Narcissus and Goldmund were mere literary ciphers.

Narcissus' inner conflicts are understated in the novel. They are not aired nearly as dramatically as those of Goldmund. But they take their toll in Narcissus' physical appearance; they give him the look of an ascetic. Although Narcissus has "two souls" within him, he is not, however, like Faust. Whereas Faust hurries through every phase of his life chasing his vision of a more satisfying future, Narcissus for all his foresight lives in the present. He knows he will be Abbot of Mariabronn. Yet this foreknowledge does not mean that his goal consumes him.

He does not pursue it with fierce singlemindedness. It simply comes to him in due course. Time does not have a hold on him as it does on Goldmund whose life style and successes depend on youthfulness. Narcissus is not the victim of time, and therefore present and future are not in conflict in him, as is the case in Faust. In not being subject to time - one of the reasons why Narcissus cannot "die" - Narcissus is not a typically Western type, but, strangely enough, in his efforts to nurture and sustain the self, which he does by contemplation, he is not unlike Faust.

## Goldmund

In contrast to Narcissus, Goldmund lives in time. It is his enemy. Like Faust, he suffers from the knowledge that all things are transient. But as a lover, Goldmund is not the typical Western "Don Juan" figure. Don Juan is propelled to find the one and only woman in every new female. Goldmund, on the other hand, does not yearn for any past or future lover in the arms of his girls. He finds the "right" woman every time. Don Juan never finds her. Thus, as a lover, Goldmund is not a seeker, he is a finder. In this century there are few Western writers of stature who present successful heroes. Hesse's great appeal to the young can in part be explained by the fact that some of his **protagonists** find fulfillment. He seems to provide answers. But they are highly individualistic answers and apply to literary figures. They are Hesse's, the idealist's formulation of what human beings might be, not so much of what they are. It also must not be overlooked that the end of the novel spells as much sadness as happiness. For although the two friends find a large degree of fulfillment in their spheres, and although Goldmund dies happy, as friends they cannot truly meet. In this sense the novel is typically Western - or perhaps typically German. Pain, unhappiness, is part of the Faustian ethos. Goethe remarked that there were no happy days in his life after his years of adolescence. He made the statement with pride, not with self-pity. This pain is the yearning to make one's vision, be it ever so unattainable in the absolute sense, or the better or missing side of one's personality, become more or even absolutely real. It involves a frustrated dialectic. Although there is no frustration in Goldmund's love life, there is yearning for the opposite pole in his personality. When he leads an urban existence, he longs for the open road. When he is a wayfarer, he misses the order and discipline that an artist's life entails. Ultimately, Goldmund cannot live with or without the Narcissus world. He is, then, a curious amalgam of a non-active hero, to whom all things come although he travels far and wide, and a Faustian type who yearns for whatever pole of his personality is underexpressed at a given time.

# NARCISSUS AND GOLDMUND

## CRITICISM

### THE CRITICS HAVE THEIR SAY ON NARCISSUS AND GOLDMUND

The chorus of criticism on *Narcissus and Goldmund* is highly dissonant. It includes praise and severe censure, some obvious misjudgment and, of course, much very useful information. An attempt will be made here to present a fair sampling of the spectrum. The student will find some questions in the Guide To Further Study directed at the critical voices presented in this chapter. Thereby he is encouraged to subject them to a critical hearing himself.

Lyrical-Wearisome-Profound is the book in Mark Boulby's assessment. His analysis is the most extensive among the serious critics of *Narcissus and Goldmund*. It is to him a lyrical novel and Hesse a Neo-romanticist:

> A lyricist disguised as a novelist, Hesse might be defined as a self-confessed Romantic epigone who yearns for raw truth, for the purity of absolute self-disclosure...

In *Narcissus and Goldmund*, Boulby feels, Hesse wishes to overcome the lyric impulse. Boulby finds the attempt laudable but chides the novel for repetitiousness of **theme** that betrays a weariness of the esthetic imagination in Hesse. In that it combines biographical confession with lyric and religious impulses, Boulby advises that *Narcissus and Goldmund* "should primarily be understood as the conversion of confession into music, into cadences, and as the refugeseeking of the disappointed mystic in art."

The Genuine Article: A Beautiful Medieval Tapestry is the novel to Ernst Robert Curtius, the most prestigious and universal scholar to have written on *Narcissus and Goldmund*. He is most unequivocal on this novel, considering it Hesse's most "beautiful book":

> The whole thing is a wonderfully colorful picture of the German Middle Ages, fusing Romanticism and Realism…without didacticism, without problems…. No work of Hesse's has a greater claim to entering into the repertory of our literature. It is a thoroughly German book, untouched by the seduction of the East which already enmeshed the writer at that time.

Curtius, for all his praise of *Narcissus and Goldmund*, does not regard Hesse as a great writer. He is to him too subjective and caught up in his own biographical experiences in his other works.

Herr Doktor Hesse commands high praise from H. David-Schwarz. He considers *Narcissus and Goldmund* a psychological masterpiece, a convincing and readable case history. As a work of literature, it impresses him far less. It is to him tediously **didactic**, a compilation of epigonal fragments.

Hesse?: Vastly Overrated says Karlheinz Deschner, a German journalist and venomous iconoclast. In fact, he does not rate Hesse an artist at all, but a hand-me-down romanticist and hack. If there are weaknesses in Hesse, however, Deschner does put his finger on some of them, dispensing caustic commentary. One example is his evaluation of the **episode** that finds Goldmund trying to seduce Lydia: "Gently he stroked her knees, touched her sex ever so delicately and begged: 'My little flower, we could be so very happy. Will you not let me?'" Deschner: "Something such as this, with its idyllic veneer - one could almost call it anacreontic, playful - today affects us as pale, polished, syrupy, sentimental; it is painfully gauche." In addition, Deschner finds fault with Goldmund and Narcissus as characters: "Such people don't exist, they are constructions, creatures of thought, not of life; they come from the test tube of the brain, in order to embody the Faustian two-souls-formula of their creator."

Not Too Bad - For a Hesse Novel is D. J. Enright's verdict. He objects to Hesse's ponderousness and explicitness, but is impressed with his unerring good sense for depicting the physical and erotic. Enright sees *Narcissus and Goldmund* as Hesse's best novel: "Where generally Hesse's persons merely dent the walls of the ivory tower on the inside, here Hesse breaks clean through them and goes on what seems a real journey through a reasonably real medieval Germany." But even in *Narcissus and Goldmund* Enright sees the characteristic liabilities of Hesse's craft:

> His easy, sure touch in physical matters (what impresses is the goodness of the eroticism, its naturalness, indeed its pleasurableness) contrasts oddly with his overheated metaphysicality, his lascivious loose talk about destiny, the abyss, the longing for death and the All.

Enright agrees with Ziolkowski, whom he reviews in the same article, that Goldmund and Narcissus as characters are not equally balanced representatives of their respective spheres: "the balance of the novel tips in favor of nature, art, action, and the flesh, as against spirit, religion, contemplation, and asceticism."

Don't Count Narcissus Out. George Wallis Field does not see any major flaws in the schematic balances of *Narcissus and Goldmund*. As a novel it deserves neither high praise nor rejection: "Misunderstanding [by the critics] may lie at the root of both censure and encomia." Field emphasizes that the pole of Narcissus is strengthened by its recurrence in Goldmund's mind and life through symbol:

> Hesse manages to have Narziss recur in Goldmund's thoughts from time to time; and when Goldmund turns to sculpture, it is the figure of Narziss he is intent on creating. If, however, the Narcissus motif underlies all those water or mirror reflections in Goldmund's vagabondage, then a strengthened claim can be made for the subconscious presence of Narziss during his physical absence.

I Like it, But I Have Done Better, says Hesse on *Narcissus and Goldmund*. He disagreed with the readers who preferred it to *Steppenwolf*. But rereading it 25 years after its publication he found that nothing in the book moved him to either censure or regret. No doubt Hesse reacts in this statement to the critics who had belittled *Narcissus and Goldmund*.

Wild Stabs in the Dark, or should one describe Stephen Koch's remarks as critical thrusts? There are so many startling assessments in Koch's article that even the most placid reader of Hesse will feel challenged. Koch speaks of the "corny tenderness" of *Narcissus and Goldmund.* It is to him "a rage in praise of heterosexuality." The novel, he asserts, "is about wanting women ...screwing girls...that is the substance of the book." "Hesse's habitual dualism is trivial academic rubbish." The "book's best moments are... blasted with chaos." Koch finds in Hesse a disparity between low intellectual and high esthetic capabilities. "Despite his faults, Hesse is a graceful and generally unpretentious artist." Hesse's appeal to the cultists is to Koch "explained by Hesse's irretrievably adolescent" thought. Koch also presents American readers with the amazing news that in Germany it is an open secret that Hesse was an overt homosexual all his life.

Just Another Romantic Tale is Louis Kronenberger's notion of *Narcissus and Goldmund.* He sees it as a form of the historical novel, appreciates its lyrical quality, but denies it any claim to modernity in form and psychological insight:

> [There] is nothing modern or Freudian, but [there is] the flavor of the Middle Ages when the flesh and the spirit - though at odds in the theological sense - somehow coalesced in the human one. Hesse's mysticism has no depth to it and gives no feeling of communicating authentic experience, but it is touched enough with poetry.

German Romanticism is Alive and Well in Hesse, thinks Joseph Mileck. He feels that *Narcissus and Goldmund* may be singled out by posterity to be Hesse's best effort. To him it is very modern in its psychological depth and belongs to German Romanticism's best tradition of story-telling. It is in *Narcissus and Goldmund,* besides *Siddhartha* and *Magister Ludi,* that Hesse, according to Mileck, managed:

> ...to extricate himself sufficiently from his engrossment with his own immediate, personal problems to enable him to mold his art with that care necessary to insure it, beyond all doubt, against the wear of time and to give it some of the more universal implications inherent in all truly great art.

Upward and Onward is clearly the direction the novel's **protagonists** take for Ernst Rose. He sees the structure of *Narcissus and Goldmund* determined by the concept of stages in human development. To Rose, Narcissus is portrayed as having an advanced state of development from the beginning. "Yet we know that in spite of his relative maturity he has by no means reached the ultimate stage of sainthood. Even in the end Narcissus has not achieved perfection; he is still on the way to it." Goldmund's life, according to Rose, is framed by Narcissus' and develops in three stages. It moves from innocence of nature, including Goldmund's first love affairs, to a conflict between spirit and flesh, i.e., good and evil. The murder of Viktor marks his fall from Grace. Then, in Rose's view:

> ...follows the conscious dedication to accepted evaluations of life and work under the guidance of Master Nicholas. There is just as conscious abandonment during the period of the Black Death and the episode with the governor's courtesan. Acquiescence to God's will is begun by Goldmund's turn to Mariabronn, but it is not achieved without major struggles. The vision of reintegration and a regained "innocence" comes to Goldmund only in his dying hours.

Rose also feels that Hesse "brings the world of the late Middle Ages vividly alive.... The touching innocence of medieval men and women, the simple piety of medieval art, the unspoiled character of the medieval landscape, are ever present in ever changing images."

Not in Top Form is Theodore Ziolkowski's verdict of Hesse's writing in *Narcissus and Goldmund*. Ziolkowski is convinced it is the most imperfect of Hesse's later works. Its public success he sees as related to its artistic shortcomings. The title of the first translation, *Death and the Lover*, refers only to the erotic hero, Goldmund. Narcissus is ignored in the title and this, according to Ziolkowski, accurately reflects the structural onesidedness of the novel. Though it was Hesse's intention to portray the equally balanced poles of nature and spirit, he failed, in Ziolkowski's opinion. The German readers, in reaction to whom Hesse insisted that Narcissus indeed had equal billing, as well as the original translator, correctly saw Goldmund as the novel's erotic hero:

> It was Hesse's intention to portray, through the dual figures of the German title, the equally balanced poles of nature and spirit, which approach each other and reach a synthesis in the realm of art. This theme, which is clearly developed in the novel, fits organically into the development of Hesse's thought. But as fiction - as plot and structure - the work fails to express the theme adequately. The reader senses a rift between content and form, a rift indicated by the English title...

# NARCISSUS AND GOLDMUND

## ESSAY QUESTIONS AND ANSWERS

Question: *Narcissus and Goldmund* has been referred to as a "picaresque novel." What justification is there in this label?

(A picaresque novel is the life story of a rogue, a clever and amusing adventurer of low social class who makes his way by tricks and roguery rather than by honorable industry. His immoral rascality manages somehow - even when he takes up with thieves - to fall a hair breadth short of actual criminality. Usually, it is a novel of the road, and the hero wanders from place to place as well as from job to job. When the story ends, the picaro has learned to conform outwardly to the ways of society.)

Answer: Calling *Narcissus and Goldmund* a "picaresque novel" presupposes that we read it largely as those critics suggest who see this novel as a lopsided affair favoring Goldmund as a hero. It must be admitted that the general intelligent reader who approaches the book without either concern for how Hesse himself saw his brainchild or heed for its substrata of symbolism is convinced he is reading primarily the story of one Goldmund. Admittedly, Goldmund is ennobled by his friendship with the reserved and aloof Narcissus as well as by his occasional gluttonous cravings for art, but aside from these two elements, he lacks refinement. Goldmund never stoops to work except when he sculptures, which he largely does for self-gratification. He could, in fact, possibly be seen as rather a base fellow. Goldmund is carried from **episode** to episode like a cork from wave to wave. He does manifest the buoyancy of the picaro who withstands the most amazing perils and comes out unscathed. Who but Goldmund could rummage through a pestilential hut full of corpses without becoming infected. He lives by his lucky star and is at one time aided by the ribald wits of the one authentic and full blown picaro in the novel, the greedy Viktor.

Goldmund is a Don Juanesque picaro. The number of women he beds exceeds the fondest dreams of undergraduate types of the generation now over thirty. As one bold critic of over thirty has shrewdly observed, *Narcissus and Goldmund* is not at all about the lofty struggle between the concepts of spirit and soul, or some such pretentious powers that be, but about "screwing women." He gloats over the fact that Goldmund gets plenty.

There has been a general fascination with the rogue in the tradition of Western literature. The reader can identify with a fellow who can get away with bucking City Hall, with beating the system. But here lies the rub. Assuming that *Narcissus and Goldmund* is a picaresque novel, we would have to ask ourselves, what system is Goldmund trying to beat, what City Hall is he trying to buck. Hesse does not provide one that we would want to aid Goldmund in overcoming. There are no societal forces worthy of our serious aversion in the novel. Even Master Niklaus' guild remains nebulous; it never becomes visible enough to amount to any kind of a threat to Goldmund. His shenanigans with the knight's daughters perhaps come closest to the notion of the picaro catching a free ride. But Goldmund does not in any way intend to or manage to upset the castle as he also does not disturb the supreme symbol of authority in the novel, the cloister. On the contrary, often Goldmund and the representatives of the establishment seem to be in partnership with one another. Instead of horsewhipping or impaling the lout, the knight is just deeply grieved that Goldmund did his best to seduce his daughters. He leads Goldmund so far out of the castle that we suspect he might be afraid that poor Goldmund will lose his way in the cruel world. Narcissus even suggests that under certain circumstances, Goldmund would be justified in burning the cloister down. Goldmund, in fact, has a tragic love affair going with the system. The only problem is that his soul is so shaped that he cannot consummate his love.

Goldmund lacks a quintessential feature of the picaro. He is not of low birth. Therefore he does not have the gutsy animosity towards those in charge that is necessary for the genuine rogue. He is an aristocrat, half by birth and fully so by inclination. Thus he appropriately does not really go in for skirt-chasing and occasional thievery. He has a loftier aim; he wishes to catch the one woman behind all women, the Great Mother. Goldmund, in fact, comes close to succeeding; the strapping Agnes is every inch a Great Mother figure.

On second reading, it is just impossible to see Goldmund as a true picaro, notwithstanding the fact that he gets in trouble and miraculously out of it again or that he inhabits the picaro's most comfortable stomping ground, the Middle Ages. The symbolic level, showing the connectedness of all the loose episodes, is his quest of the Great Mother. Goldmund is not ultimately a drifter though his quest is largely subconscious. On the conscious level we have a tension-laden yet affirmative dialectic with the "system." Unlike the picaro, though, social barriers could not keep Goldmund from joining the world of Narcissus. Goldmund, though unconscious of it, sets up an antinomal structure to the cloister, to order and mind. When the last sparks in the dialectic between him and Narcissus are gone, they nonetheless continue to singe Narcissus who admits that Goldmund's world represents a successful challenge to his own. No picaro ever triumphed on such a scale.

Question: How can *Narcissus and Goldmund* be defended as good literature?

Answer: In a certain perspective *Narcissus and Goldmund* can be quite easily defended as good literature. This perspective involves a view of art to which every young devotee of Hesse would subscribe: art is great if it speaks to a whole generation in terms that seem valid beyond the given era. There are, indeed, sufficient universals in Hesse that are likely to be meaningful to the earnest seeker of spiritual values for years to come.

This view parallels a fundamental notion of Marxist literary criticism. To the Marxist, the esthetics of a work of art are simply meaningless unless they are part and parcel of the social consciousness inherent in the art work. Thus every work of art should have cultural relevance and be judged esthetically by this criterion. Needless to say, Hesse's works do not qualify as Socialist **Realism** nor is the concept of individualism that Hesse propounds greatly admired by the Marxist critics. (Hesse's longing for a Third Kingdom in *Steppenwolf* and *Magister Ludi*, however, is viewed with sympathy because the millennium is felt to have arrived in the Socialist world.)

Many critics in the Western world, however, flirt with the view that esthetics is bound up with social impact. Few are willing to call Hesse's books outright trash any more in view of his stupendous popularity among those who are the hope of the future. Therefore many assume a position of ambivalence.

Curiously enough, calling *Narcissus and Goldmund* a mixed bag of literary goods may come close to a valid judgment even on the "old fashioned" grounds of Imminent Criticism. Forgetting how popular Hesse is and following the great critic, E. R. Curtius, who wished that a work of art be seen in terms of its thematic correspondences and its structural craftsmanship, we look at the book as such and come to the conclusion that Hesse succeeds in some aspects and fails in others. The final question is, does the good outweigh the bad?

The central **theme** of *Narcissus and Goldmund* is self-realization. It is projected by plot, motif, symbol and **metaphor**. The plot carries Goldmund far afield. He finds himself only in the end. Narcissus, however, stays where he is, in the cloister, for in terms of his consciousness, he is always what he shall be at the end of his life. Narcissus' form of being is underscored by **metaphor**. There is much prayer and solitude connected with him because he is a contemplative type. Narcissus, however, is not supported nearly as extensively by **metaphor** as is Goldmund.

The motifs and symbols that convey and support Goldmund's form of self-realization are determined by the very nature of his development. They all are part of and point to the supreme symbol of Goldmund's sphere, the Great Mother. His continual love affairs are an appropriate motif, as is the motif of recurrence since it reflects the eternal sameness and also the transitoriness of the Mother World. Symbols related to the Mother World are the water, fish, the horse, the dogs. These are the lines within Goldmund's own development. Then there are the **metaphors** that connect him to Narcissus' and the Father World. The notion of repetition is not emphasized in Narcissus' and Goldmund's relationship; they actually meet only twice. Since Goldmund's love for Narcissus is mainly spiritual, it does not need renewal by physical contact. The Father symbols are the cloister to which he returns, the world of the burgher, the world of the knight and that of Rebekka.

The Father World is forever with Goldmund. He is tied to it by love and longing. Art, which can "begin with the sensual and can aspire to the highest level of the spiritual," is the great symbol of mediation between the two worlds.

All these formal strands are woven in intricate repeat-patterns ranging from the boldest colors of external experience to the shaded lines of the state of the soul. There can be no question that Hesse managed to create an impressive thematic structure. But unfortunately, he occasionally does lapse into various keys of falsetto. Where he ought to use the bold colors of sensuality, he is soulful (as in the **episode** quoted once before). "Gently he stroked her knees, touched her sex ever so delicately and begged, 'My little flower, we could be so very happy. Will you not let me?'" (The original is even more sentimental; "Er streichelte sachte ihre Knie, und indem er ganz zart ihre Scham beruhrte, bat er: 'Blumchen, wir konnten so sehr glucklich sein! Darf ich nicht?'") On the other hand, when he should be soulful and subtle, he becomes on occasion ponderously explicit, as when Narcissus tells Goldmund what the difference is between them. "Your home is the earth, ours is the world of ideas.... You are an artist; I am a thinker. You sleep at the breast of the mother; I wake in the desert...your dreams are of girls; mine of boys..."

In *Narcissus and Goldmund*, Hesse has done full justice to the demands of sophisticated literary design; however, he shows some shoddy workmanship in detail. *Narcissus and Goldmund* is a good novel. There are, however, to this reader too many flaws of stylistic detail to call it great.

Question: Is Goldmund a cop-out?

Answer: Although there are some critics who find fault with *Narcissus and Goldmund*, they rarely indict it directly for lacking a social consciousness. But at times there is an implicit social verdict in their perspective. If we think of *Narcissus and Goldmund* as an important novel, the remark that it is all about "screwing women" or the insistence that it is a "beautiful lyrical novel" will have to make us uncomfortable. We ask ourselves, how can a serious book in the twentieth century completely ignore the all-pervasive social forces in the lives of men and still be an authentic reflection of our times. There is no questioning the fact that *Narcissus and Goldmund* abstains from dealing with the social and economic issues which we customarily identify as being the primary forces that shape contemporary man.

In defense of the novel, we would have to say that the primary social forces in the Middle Ages took the form of religion rather than economics. Unfortunately, however, religion is only a metaphorical constituent of the novel. The cloister is a symbol of the spirit, but true Christian piety or believable expressions of faith are almost completely absent. Abbot Daniel is the one exception to the rule. He evidences believable faith, worry and concern for his charges. There is the warmth in him that can strengthen bonds in the society of Mariabronn. Hesse's placing the social dimension in a minor and, what's more, unexciting figure, indicates the low priority he ascribed to social questions.

Goldmund, as a boy, is not without feelings for the society of Mariabronn. He venerates Abbot Daniel, but quickly comes under the influence of Narcissus and has to learn that he is not meant to be a societal creature. Narcissus is in a sense an extremely sinister influence on Goldmund. He convinces Goldmund that he would not be happy in the cloister. One might psychologize a bit and suspect that Narcissus sees a threat in Goldmund not merely to his own personality type but to his ambition as a leader in the cloister. If Abbot Daniel were able to be an effective leader, Goldmund, who shared some characteristics with the Abbot, could have become an even more effective one. Narcissus forces Goldmund, the extravert, this man with great potential for social action, into the role of a misanthrope and social cynic. If Goldmund is to be seen as a cop-out from the cloister, this is the juncture at which he should have asserted himself against Narcissus.

But Goldmund accepts the perspective of himself that Narcissus offers; however, he does so with some reservations. He wishes to stay with some of the girls he meets early in his wanderings and so form a more lasting liaison even though Narcissus had instructed him by prophecy that he would not stay with one girl for long. Only during the period of absolute chaos, the plague, does Goldmund develop a societal sense. But it is a means to an end, a game that will end as soon as he tires of it. Although Goldmund indicates that he intends to leave Lene someday, he remains with her while she is dying of the plague. But his compassion for her cannot be divorced from his fascination with death. Thus it is not primarily a social act. Goldmund resorts to no philosophical perspective, to no article of faith which would take the sting out of the horror of this death. It is a "shocking scene" to him, but it is also "fateful." It is another step on the route to getting to the very core of the experience of life and death. At the end of his life, Goldmund is fully willing to accept life as leading to death. He has looked into the abyss, and he has accepted death as its dark content. Goldmund, then, is only a cop-out in a narrow societal sense. But he is anything but a cop-out in his relentless quest for experience. From the view of the abyss, he gleaned both the raw courage of the will to survive and also the acceptance of death that is born of the willingness to live without illusions.

# NARCISSUS AND GOLDMUND

## TOPICS FOR RESEARCH AND CRITICISM

........................................................

### COMING TO TERMS WITH THE CRITICS

The Title of *Narcissus and Goldmund* Gives the Heroes Equal Billing. Does the Text Support the Title?

Narcissus on the Road to Sainthood. The Notion of Perfection in *Narcissus and Goldmund*.

*Narcissus and Goldmund* and the Middle Ages.

Hesse's Lyrical Style in *Narcissus and Goldmund*. Asset or Liability?

*Narcissus and Goldmund* and the German Romantic Tradition of Storytelling.

Goldmund and the Oedipus Complex.

Narcissus and Goldmund *as a* **Didactic** *Novel*.

Are There Eastern Influences in *Narcissus and Goldmund*?

How Justified Is the Critical Charge of Metaphysicality and Explicitness Leveled against *Narcissus and Goldmund?*

Narcissus and Goldmund *as an Erotic Novel.*

Can We Accept Hesse's Judgment That *Steppenwolf* Is a Better Book Than *Narcissus and Goldmund*?

Is It Valid to Speak of the Structure of *Narcissus and Goldmund* as Following the Pattern of Innocence, Fall, and Redemption?

*Narcissus and Goldmund* as a Reflection of Hesse's Life and Development.

Does Hesse Successfully Integrate the Biographical Elements in the Structure of *Narcissus and Goldmund*? Compare *Narcissus and Goldmund* with *Steppenwolf* in this Perspective.

Could Goldmund Be a Mouthpiece for Hesse's Religious Beliefs?

## COMPARATIVE TOPICS: GENERAL LITERATURE

Goldmund and Faust.

Goldmund and Don Juan.

Goldmund and the Wandering Jew.

Narcissus and Faust.

The Technique of Equal Prominence of Two or More **Protagonists** in Hesse, Dos Passos, Gide, and Huxley.

Goldmund and Grass' *Goldmaulchen.*

Shakespeare's **Sonnet** *147* and Goldmund's *Love of the Great Mother.*

The Apollonian vs. the Dionysian in *Narcissus and Goldmund* and Thomas Mann's *Death in Venice.*

The Polarity of Spirit and Soul in *Narcissus and Goldmund* and Goethe's *Faust.*

## COMPARATIVE TOPICS: HESSE'S OWN WORKS

Goldmund and Siddhartha.

Goldmund and Berthold.

The Symbols of the Spirit: Mariabronn in *Narcissus and Goldmund* and Castalia in *Magister Ludi.*

The Artist **Theme** in *Narcissus and Goldmund, Klingsor's Last Summer,* and *Magister Ludi.*

The Friendship **Theme** in *Narcissus and Goldmund* and *Demian.*

Homosexuality in Hesse's Works.

## RELEVANCE TOPICS

Hesse's Portrayal of Women in *Narcissus and Goldmund.*

Ethics of Love in *Narcissus and Goldmund.*

Art as Therapy of the Soul in *Narcissus and Goldmund.*

Goldmund's and Narcissus' Situation Ethics.

Hesse's Outsider Figures: Harry Haller, Emil Sinclair, Goldmund.

The Outsider in Hesse's *Narcissus and Goldmund* and Goethe's *Werther.*

The Outsider in Hesse's *Narcissus and Goldmund* and Thomas Mann's *Tonio Kroger.*

*Narcissus and Goldmund*: A Guide to Human Happiness?

## MISCELLANEOUS TOPICS

Animal Symbolism in *Narcissus and Goldmund.*

Water Symbolism in *Narcissus and Goldmund.*

Role of the Virgin Mary in *Narcissus and Goldmund.*

Nature in *Narcissus and Goldmund.*

Hesse's Attitude Toward the Jews.

Time Schemes in *Narcissus and Goldmund*.

Open and Closed Spaces in *Narcissus and Goldmund*.

Hesse and Jung.

Hesse and Bachofen.

The Theories of Art in *Narcissus and Goldmund* and Schopenhauer.

www.ingramcontent.com/pod-product-compliance
Lightning Source LLC
LaVergne TN
LVHW012058070526
838200LV00070BA/2969